LEGACY

LEGACY

THE SCOTS IRISH IN AMERICA

Alister McReynolds

AMBASSADOR INTERNATIONAL
Greenville, South Carolina • Belfast, Northern Ireland

- for Eileen -

ISBN 978-1-935507-01-7

Ambassador Publications
a division of
Ambassador Productions Ltd.
Providence House
Ardenlee Street,
Belfast,
BT6 8QJ
Northern Ireland
www.ambassador-productions.com

Emerald House
427 Wade Hampton Blvd.
Greenville
SC 29609, USA
www.emeraldhouse.com

Contents

ACKNOWLEDGMENTS

THANKS are due to:

Victor Blease for getting me interested at school.

Gillian Graham for being a superb Editor-in-Chief.

Willy Drennan for sharing information on Nova Scotia and The Fighting McCooks

John Knox for sharing material about his ancestor-John Armoy Knox.

In the state of Maine I owe a considerable debt to the 'Mainers' involved in MUSP (Maine Ulster Scots Project) , particularly John and Val Mann and Bill McKeen. Also in Maine I am particularly grateful to Bill Barry of the Maine Historical Society who has allowed me access to his unpublished thesis on the McLellan and Patten families and who went out of his way and 'gave above the call' to assist me on my quest for the Scots Irish in Maine.

Professor John Wilson, Director of the Institute of Ulster Scots Studies, has been a source of constant support and encouragement.

John Ross and Janice Chahib for their technical support and advice.

My elder son Michael McReynolds for being an excellent travelling companion and for taking many of the photographs.

Tom Arbuthnot and William Dinsmoor for providing material on New England poet Robert Dinsmoor- an ancestor of the latter.

Dr Tim Campbell of the St Patrick centre Downpatrick who has opened doors that have allowed others to see this work.

Bob Hayes and the members of Lower Broomhedge Ulster Scots Society for their always infectious enthusiasm.

George Patton and Billy Kennedy for their encouragement and for allowing publication of these chapters , many of which have appeared in various versions in The Ulster Scot and on Ulster Scots Agency websites.

Paddy Fitzgerald and Brian Lambkin for readily making available the resources of the Centre for Migration Studies in Omagh Co. Tyrone.

Staff in the Public Library in Moira Co. Down , University of Ulster Library at Jordanstown, Public Records Office for Northern Ireland at Balmoral Avenue Belfast.

David Torrans of 'No Alibis' Bookshop Belfast for his encouragement and his 'insider views' on American writing.

The Ulster Scots Agency for a generous study grant that allowed research in New England, particularly in the State of Maine.

Mrs E Fulton for information on Robert Fulton.

Staff at Leach Library, Londonderry, N.H.

Staff at Museum in Belfast, Maine.

Doug and Grace Boyce of Franklin, Virginia.

Jean and Tom McReynolds for their encouragement.

Foreword From America

John Mann - Chairman of MUSP

THE fascination remains.

Sometimes it is admiration or pride. Sometimes it is curiosity and a hunger to understand ourselves and the root stock from which our culture has grown — to understand how and why we have prospered, failed, struggled, persevered and spread ever westward across North America — to understand how individuals and families managed their lives and their times in a dramatically changing and often dangerous world. It has been nearly three hundred years since the first great exodus from Ulster Plantation in the North of Ireland to the New World began, but the fascination remains.

In the sixty years prior to the American Revolution, some quarter of a million people departed Ulster in hope of better opportunities in America. The circumstances that pushed them to consider leaving and the ideas that pulled them onward have been explored and written about with some detail. Those circumstances will be re-examined as time goes on and new archives are explored, but for many of us, the root of our fascination is with the people themselves.

Northern Ireland today looks westward and wonders at the rise of American politics and culture, and at the stories lived out by her sons and daughters. North America looks eastward to the small collection of counties that is Northern Ireland and wonders what manner of people is this who played such a defining role in their heritage and history — and the fascination remains.

Our curiosity has new and previously inconceivable tools to help us satisfy or feed the flame of our fascination. The great western ocean and the vast reaches of America's forests and prairies no longer separate Ulster from her grandchildren. The obstacles of distance and time are erased. The internet opens doors to archives. Email transfers thoughts and data at the speed of light. Travel between our two homelands no longer means a lifetime of separation from home and kin. The development of these tools is far more than an opportunity to indulge our curiosity: it is an opportunity to reinvigorate the sense of family and friendship that is forged from sharing a common heritage.

Alister McReynolds has taken the time to research and report on the lives of various people who lived in and dealt with turbulent times — people who grappled with the difficulties and opportunities of a young America and who helped to define her character. In this book he presents us with a collection of their stories — stories of adaptation and creativity in a rapidly changing world.

The first "five ships" (as they have come to be known) in the 1718 migration from Ulster reached the shore of North America in New England. Their passengers began settlements in the colonial frontier back country of Massachusetts, New Hampshire and the District of Maine *"...where Indians gave them a most unenviable time"* as R. J. Dickson wrote in his ground-breaking book "*Ulster Emigration to Colonial America 1718-1775.*" Their settlements were encouraged for three reasons:

first, to secure a defensive perimeter against attacks from the French and Indians:

second, to advance the claim of Britain into disputed territories:

and third, to improve property values for Massachusetts land speculators.

Holding their foothold at the "eastern frontier" meant struggling against tremendous challenges, but Maine's Ulster Scots held fast and spread, with dozens of additional settlements to follow. There were at least 32 settlements of Scots and Scots-Irish, prior to the American Revolution, in Maine alone. This particular branch of the Ulster Diaspora has until recently been much overlooked in the general discourse of the "Scotch-Irish" influence on American history.

In 2006 the Maine Ulster-Scots Project (MUSP) was created by the Saint Andrews Society of Maine. MUSP was created to promote awareness of Maine's Scots-Irish heritage and to gather and archive the stories of Maine's first 'Ulster-Scots' families through the time of the American Revolution. One of the first people from Northern Ireland to find the MUSP website and inquire into our mission was Alister McReynolds. His interest in our history and his helpful enthusiasm for our work soon led to great things. Alister has spent time in Maine and New Hampshire researching our records, viewing our historic sites and promoting our mission. He has traipsed the cemeteries of Maine's colonial period settlements and paused to consider the empty lands where homes and families of Ulster immigrants were destroyed during the French and Indian wars. Alister has also brought his perspective and research to the lectern as keynote speaker at the first annual Maine Celtic Celebration in Belfast, Maine — *Belfast*, whose name was chosen instead of *Londonderry* at the toss of a coin.

My wife Val and I have in turn spent time in Northern Ireland pursuing the same objectives there. With Alister as our guide and advisor, we were able to find the burial sites of our Anderson family ancestors at Aghaloo, the remains of Mann Castle near Six Mile Cross and, in the vestry records of St. Colum's Cathedral, the vital statistics of the Man(n) family, predating the siege of Londonderry. We also spent time in Ballymoney which is the ancestral home of Val's Maybury family as well as many other Maine families. The most significant by-product of this pursuit has been the great friendships forged along the way.

Several articles have now been produced regarding Maine's founding Ulster families and several more regarding the connection of Maine families within Ulster. Two of those pieces appear in this book. They are stories of the hard working common people of Maine's frontier who pulled together successful lives from the raw materials that surrounded them and the extended family that supported them.

Ulster's connection with Maine has spanned the generations and has now been revived, in no small part through the efforts of Maine's Senator George Mitchell and his involvement in the Northern Ireland peace process. Indeed, Senator Mitchell has written in his introduction to the book *"They Change Their Sky: The Irish In Maine"* in regards to Maine's Scots-Irish *"My work for the peace process and reconciliation in Northern Ireland has taught me that historical amnesia never succeeds in the long term and, therefore, it is imperative to chronicle the experience of this group..."*

This volume of ***'Legacy'*** gives us a look back at the challenges faced by the shared ancestors of Ulster and North

America. Learning how real people adapted during times of great physical and cultural transition is often inspiring but always fascinating. Let us take this opportunity to reacquaint ourselves with our shared family tree and rekindle the bond of friendship that comes from a common heritage and blood memory.

John T. Mann, PLS
Chairman, Maine Ulster Scots Project
Saint Andrews Society of Maine

FOREWORD FROM ULSTER

Professor John Wilson
Director, Institute of Ulster Scots Studies, University of Ulster

AMERICA is known as a melting-pot of cultures and identities; from the original Native American peoples, through the myriad European identities, to the more recent influx of Mexican and other South American cultural groups. Yet if one truly wants to understand America and the Americans, one must pay attention to a group of people little mentioned, and perhaps even less understood. One American Professor has referred to this group as 'the people with no name', whom he then, paradoxically, identifies as the Scots Irish and Ulster Scots. Both designations are not easily delimited, but both have enough elements of descriptive common sense to be easily understood. These are the people, originally form Scotland, who later named as their home Ulster, before then moving on again to the New World where they would become the first frontiers people, and lead the way into the new lands of America geographically, culturally, politically and militarily.

In his new book 'Legacy' Alister McReynolds explores who these people were, where they came from, and what they achieved. He does so in a refreshingly clear and accessible style, ranging far and wide across, amongst other areas, religion, philosophy, business, slavery, cookery and cowboys. It is through the actions of individuals and their achievements, beliefs and inventions, that we see the way in which the links that bind Ulster, Scotland and the United States may be traced across the generations. In this way McReynolds constrains chronology so that we may dip in and out of the stories, gathering insights and information, and marvelling at the seemingly unparalleled impact of these people.

McReynolds has a clear feeling for the generational connections he is accessing and highlighting: these are his people, his ancestors. For many others in Scotland, Ulster, the USA and elsewhere these stories will generate similar pride and interest. But even for readers of other ethnically diverse backgrounds there is much to marvel at in this book. There is also much that generates surprise, and there is much to ponder- is it really true that the American enlightenment and the war of independence were driven by a Scots Irish stubbornness and resolute belief in the freedom of the individual? Is it possible that the culinary revolution of the Deep South of the United States is built on a little sauce mixed by an Ulsterman? Is it possible that the greatest capitalist nation on the planet learned much of its business from Ulster Scots immigrants? The answer to these and many other questions you may not have considered before lies within the covers of McReynolds book.

Professor John Wilson
Director, Institute of Ulster Scots Studies
University of Ulster

Introduction

'We believe as you do that we actually built this country'. So said President Woodrow Wilson addressing a Scots Irish audience and speaking about the contribution of Scots Irish people to the building of America. I've always liked this quotation by Woodrow Wilson and yet my basic intelligence tells me that it could never be absolutely true. Obviously the building of America has been the work of people of many different ethnic origins. Although Woodrow Wilson's claim may seem exaggerated, I think I liked the fact that it presented an alternative vision of the Scots Irish in America as people who played a role very different from that of the image of the indolent and ignorant hillbilly who gave little to America other than 'moonshine whiskey', or as one who was juxtaposed against the God- fearing Calvinist who adhered to an almost impossibly rigid code of behaviour. Rather the key image in Wilson's vision was that of 'building' the country. In this series of portraits I have tried to present Scots Irish individuals who were instrumental in contributing to the building of America and consequently to the making of the modern world. I have also chosen to portray individuals like Ellen Glasgow whose creativity was born out of the tension of struggling against strict and unforgiving moral control on the part of her conventional Scots Irish father.

Having gently challenged one stereotype I was keen also to demonstrate that whilst Appalachia was central to Scots Irish settlement, particularly amongst those who settled after 1730, I wanted to show that the Scots Irish also made a considerable mark on the ethnicity of states outside the Appalachian Mountains, so I have been at pains to portray the Scots Irish settlements in New England, particularly that in Maine, and also beyond in Nova Scotia and in Southern Georgia and Louisiana.

Alister John McReynolds
Co. Antrim, 2009

1

Feeling Related

In the 1960's the great American novelist John Steinbeck decided to amble around the fields where his Scots Irish roots grew – to visit Mulkeraugh near Limavady in County Londonderry from whence his maternal grandfather Samuel Hamilton had journeyed to the emigrant ship. Samuel eventually peregrinated all the way to the Salinas Valley in California. Steinbeck's visit had a profound impact on the writer – "I feel related" he said and added that he found that the people generally were like his mother's brothers, in California, "in complexion and character – talented and contentious". He spoke for many Scots Irish then and still today when he said, "and that's the seat of my culture and the origin of my being and the soil of my background."

Today it is estimated that forty million Americans are of Irish origin and of these well over half are, like John Steinbeck, Scots/Irish to their core.

As their name suggests the Scots Irish are a hybrid people who were planted in the northernmost counties of Ireland in the early part of the seventeenth Century. The original concept of Planting the rebellious ungovernable province of Ulster was undoubtedly an English idea. The early negotiations, plans and preparations were drafted by the London livery companies and guilds and it wasn't until well into the year 1610 that the 'escheated' or confiscated counties west of the River Bann, which had recently been wrested from the Gaelic Earls, were planted by settlers from lowland Scotland. Prior to this the Scots had for centuries been drifting back and forward to the Eastern Counties of Antrim and Down across the narrow straits (just twenty one miles at one point) which separate Northern Ireland and Scotland. However on the matter of the Plantation – supply and demand forces had a great deal to do with this Scottish turn of events. The English were reluctant and somewhat cautious about becoming too involved in this wild landscape. The Minute – books of the London Livery Companies bristle with comments such as, "it would be very foolish to entermeddle in this busynesse, for it will be exceading chargeable". On the other hand the hungry and tough lowland Scots race found their homeland overcrowded and needed the space and the opportunity to live and worship as they pleased. The chance to settle on lands in Ulster was one to be seized with both hands - even if that meant having to work "with the sworde in one hand and the Axe in thother". It was thus that the Scots Irish character was forged in the climate, landscape and during the dangerous times of seventeenth century Ulster. Subsequently no better people could have been found for carrying out the formidably difficult task of spreading a dawning western civilization to and eventually across America. Seventeen U.S. presidents have grown from this hardy grafted stock and that's an impressive blossoming in any planted bed.

And it's not just Presidents – the Scots Irish have made a huge contribution to America in a number of fields including politics, education, religion, the military, commerce, journalism and literature and in the arts and entertainment industry. They have been particularly prevalent amongst movie stars and include amongst their number – John Wayne, James Stewart, Robert Mitchum, Robert Redford and Greer Garson to name but a few.

Now more that ever before Scots Irish American 'cousins' are coming to visit the land of their fathers with its memorable landscape filled with prehistoric standing stones, dolmens, round towers, and impressive Norman castles such as those at Carrickfergus and Dundrum. More than anything else Scots Irish Americans want to walk in the footsteps of their ancestors and focus on the experiences of the Scottish settlers in Ulster and in particular the seventeenth Century Plantation . Today there are still so many sites associated with these events which are well worth visiting. It is in these ancient places that Scots Irish Americans feel closest to their "ain folk". The city of Londonderry and a walk around its still intact seventeenth Century walls is a 'must' in this regard. It was here that so many of the Scots Irish suffered during the siege of 1689. This siege was not only very significant for European history but had so much in common, including the very stock of the people, with the siege of the Alamo in Texas. It is remarkable that in the Texas stronghold the defenders were led by the Scots Irish hero Davy Crockett. In both cases those who were besieged held out for so long against all the odds. Back in Derry/Londonderry both St Colum's Cathedral with its siege mementoes and the refined beauty of the Guildhall built by the London companies evoke this crucial time in the history of the Scots Irish. Nowadays there are many colourful re-enactments of these events during the annual Maiden City Festival. Beyond

Londonderry there are other places to visit that re-create the life of a Planter. At nearby Springhill, Moneymore the very architectural structure of the Manor House is such that it seems to hold its 'arms' outstretched in a gesture of welcome . This house remains today as it was originally when the Scots Irish Conynghams a Planter family lived there for ten generations. Indeed 'Good' Will Conyngham played an important part during the siege of Derry and his blunderbuss, flintlocks and other firearms still hang in the gun room of the house. The superb costume museum on the site calls back the styles of dress of yesteryear in Northern Ireland.

At Bellaghy Bawn also in County Londonderry there is an impressive example of a 'bawn' – the type of fortified farmhouse which the Planters were compelled to build in order to house and protect themselves. This particular example was erected by Sir Baptist Jones who also built the town of Vintnerstown (now Bellaghy) around the skirt of the protective stockade. This work was carried out on behalf of the Vintners Company who were the London Guild that was appointed to this area. Bellaghy Bawn has the added attraction of featuring and displaying the original working papers of the much loved Nobel Prize winning poet – Seamus Heaney who has written so evocatively about growing up in the countryside around Bellaghy. The centre also contains a useful guide to the archaeology, history and nature of the area – including details of the Mulholland, O'Neil, Scullion, Heaney, Thomas, Conway and Connolly families who have lived in this area for centuries ranging between three and seven hundred years.

Moving west and driving through the dramatic Erne Lakeland of County Fermanagh unfolds much more evidence of the Plantation. At Castle Archdale the picturesquely situated ruins of the original Plantation Castle still stands as a fine example of the architectural design of the period and the nearby modern castle – a noble structure is still today the home of Mr. H.B. Archdale. Gustavus Hamilton built seventeenth century Monea Castle nearby and it is a magnificent ruin on a grand scale. Perhaps the best place to start in County Fermanagh however is at Enniskillen Castle which houses a number of fascinating displays including those which are dedicated to the Scots Irish regiments of the British Army which are associated with the town. These were founded in the late seventeenth Century to support the cause of William III. The Museum displays the uniforms and regalia of the 6th Inniskilling Dragoons and the Royal Inniskilling Fusiliers. Indeed the signature marching tune of these regiments is said to have been borrowed and adopted/adapted by the Scots Irish in America as the tune which inspired "The Star Spangled Banner".

But to return to the Planters for a moment however – unlike the Conynghams and the Hamiltons of our Plantation story most folk lived in very simple thatched cottages. Good examples may be seen at the Ulster American Folk Park in Omagh which is about an hour's drive from Enniskillen and also at the Ulster Folk and Transport Museum at Cultra.

2

Pioneers - The Emigration Trail

In May 1717 'The Friends Goodwill' left Larne for Boston with fifty two passengers on board. The ship arrived in September of that same year. Sea water had damaged supplies as a result of strong adverse winds which also resulted in the passengers arriving with very low food and fresh water reserves.

In some ways the unknown emigrants of this ship may be described as Ulster's Pilgrim Fathers. They certainly believed in those early days that the Calvinists of New England would make suitable neighbours and allow them a degree of religious freedom. However, the Puritans of New England did not feel tolerant towards the Scots Irish brand of Calvinism. In 1992 the Co. Antrim town of Larne unveiled a statue that says something about the nature of these original emigrants –in the sculptural scenario the father of the group carries the Bible and the young boy is carrying his shoes in the hope of 'Red Letter Days' ahead when he may wear them in the 'New World'.

One year later in 1718 Rev James McGregor led five ship loads of passengers from Londonderry, Macosquin,

Aghadowey and Coleraine. They settled in New Hampshire and named their settlement Londonderry with a Derry and an Antrim and a Hillsborough situated close by.

Reverend McGregor had fought at the siege of Derry. He took virtually his entire congregation with him to North America. He likened the Scots Irish exodus to America to that of Moses leading the chosen tribes to the Promised Land.

In the same summer another Presbyterian Minister, Rev James Woodside led over one hundred Scots Irish emigrants to America. They also arrived in Boston having sailed on the good ship 'McCallom'. Also from Londonderry in that same year roughly the same number of passengers set sail in the 'Mary and Elizabeth'. They also arrived in Boston. Many Catholics and Anglicans also left the city on the River Foyle during this period and so busy were the shipping lanes from the 'Maiden City' to give it its other name that the business of emigration became a thriving local industry. The irony of this is not lost on our citizens today but the fact is that most of the ships belonged to local businessmen. Some figures serve to make this point. In July 1729 one local merchant was quoted as claiming that as many as twenty five ships left the City that summer. The average number of passengers in each of these vessels would have been in the region of 150 for each trip. In 1759 a contemporaneous account stated that more than three thousand people had recently left from Derry and Coleraine. The Irish Customs Commissioners received a report that the number of emigrants leaving the City for America in 1772 and 1773 was in the region of six thousand people. This figure seems accurate since the Maryland Journal of October 1773 claimed 3,500 had left from Derry in the previous twelve months.

So Derry or Londonderry became a focus for emigration and of all the towns and Cities in Ulster it is perhaps here, more than anywhere else, that one can stand on the quay and scan the walls and conjure again the dreams and the plans that filled the hearts and minds of the Scots Irish emigrants of the early eighteenth century.

In 'Phase two' of eighteenth century emigration from Ulster i.e. the period after 1730, the Quakers of William Penn's 'Holy experiment' of settlement in Pennsylvania proved to be more tolerant of the brand of Calvinism practised by these Scots Irish Presbyterians than the Puritans of New England had been despite the latter having, on the face of it, more in common in doctrinal theological terms. So in this period we find Philadelphia becoming the port of embarkation and sheer proximity increasing the feasibility of a move onwards towards settlement in Appalachia.

A wall plaque on a house at the junction of High Street and Queen Street, Lurgan, Co Armagh bears modest testimony, as perhaps befits a Quaker, to James Logan who became President of the Council of Pennsylvania and who was an important catalyst in making Philadelphia Pennsylvania the very entrepôt for the Scots Irish into the United States. Not only were the Quakers more tolerant of Presbyterianism but Logan and Penn saw considerable advantage in having a buffer zone of these tough people between the pacifist Friends and the considerably less pacifist Native Americans. So it is by 1780 that we find a swathe of inland towns across the belly of Pennsylvania called 'Coleraine' and 'Londonderry' and by such like familiar Scots Irish names. However, even Logan who encouraged this trade in human livestock was surprised by its magnitude "It looks as if Ireland is to send all her inhabitants thither, for last week no less than six ships arrived, and every week two or three arrive also."

Most Scots Irish settlers in Ulster had lived on small farms. The Plantation had not produced the size of farms that the Scots settlers had anticipated and undoubtedly this was a major factor in persuading individuals to join the thronged exodus. Typical of this lonely decision is the simple snatch of a letter from James Smyth of Moycraig Co Antrim to his brother William in Philadelphia in 1836 – "In summer my horse died and I have not yet another. This has been the severest season ever I experienced in my life". Within one hundred years of the Plantation the settlers in Ulster had established a woollen and linen industry to rival that of England. The response of the English to this success was to virtually tax these industries out of existence by placing a trade embargo on Ulster exports.

The Test Act of 1703 prevented Presbyterians from holding any positions of civil authority and this was a major blow to a people who were obviously as ambitious as were the Scots Irish.

But undoubtedly the severe weather, be it extreme frost or drought, was a major factor in motivating emigration. This partly explains why the years of maximum exodus were 1717-'19, 1724-'29, 1740-'41, 1754-'55, and 1770-'75.

By the time of the first United States National census in 1790 only the English outnumbered the Scots Irish as America's largest ethnic population. When Washington assumed the role of the nation's First President those of Scots Irish ancestry living in the United States is estimated to have been well over one quarter of a million Americans.

Of the four hundred and forty two vessels which advertised sailings from the Northern Irish ports to America in the third quarter of the eighteenth century 33% left Belfast, 25% left Londonderry, 20% left Newry, 14% left Larne and 8% left Portrush. Of course the people who left didn't all come from these cities and towns since the agents for the various ships scoured the hinterland towns seeking likely recruits for the voyage. As you drive through the small market towns of Northern Ireland today it is still possible to picture the scene of these 'super salesmen' holding out the prospect of, 'a land of milk and honey,' to people shuffling between the webs of cloth and the live chickens in the local market place. We know for instance that Charles McKenzie Master of the ship 'Peace and Plenty' which sailed to Philadelphia and New York visited Ballynahinch, Lisburn and Ballymena in search of emigrants. Again the Masters of the 'Newry Assistance' and the 'Minerva' both bound for Philadelphia from Newry visited between them Coalisland and Cookstown in Co Tyrone, Banbridge, Rathfriland and Dromore in Co Down and Castledawson in Co Londonderry.

Whilst it is worth remembering that the eighteenth century ships that brought the Scots Irish to America were not passenger ships, but were rather cargo ships, conditions were not as bad generally as they were on the Irish famine ships of a century later. Delays were a problem in that the allowance of food given to individuals was usually accorded to them on the day they signed the Indenture rather than the day of sailing. Most Scots Irish went as Indentured servants and worked usually for three years at a particular trade in America. In return they were fed and clothed during the journey and provided with their 'keep' in America. Advertisements in the papers placed at the time included one for potatoes for a trip – this specified that the potatoes should be, "large, not washed. but dried in the sun and not cut in the digging". Very often rum was sold on board the ship, largely to ward off the cold, for three shillings and nine pence per gallon.

Although there may have been less disease than on the famine ships one interesting statistic – of the four vessels that sailed from Larne in 1772 two had smallpox on board.

The Ulster American Folk Park near Omagh, Co Tyrone has recreated a ship and dockside gallery that is full-size of scale and is the type of sailing ship that carried thousands of emigrants across the Atlantic. This particular venue also displays a wonderful indoor exhibition entitled "Emigrants" and is sited close to the Centre for Migration Studies where there are professionals willing and very able to assist anyone researching emigration history and the way of life of the emigrants and settlers. It is the largest museum of emigration in Europe. The key to understanding this traumatic movement of people in many cases comes back to the land with the Land Lease Taxation of 1771-'75 in Ulster being a large factor – Thirty thousand emigrants left these shores in 1775 alone.

The Ulster Folk and Transport Museum at Cultra near Holywood in Co Down holds unique material pertaining to emigration including passenger lists. Closely allied to this is the superb collection of material relating to Ulster's Maritime history including many valuable and unique artefacts pertaining to the ill-fated Titanic which sailed out of Belfast Lough just a few short miles and within clear sight of the grounds within which this award-winning Museum stands. The exhibition includes the unique collection of historic Titanic photographs which are not available anywhere else.

The enduring and almost instinctive movement of the eighteenth century emigrants was westward as had been that of the Planters from Scotland a hundred years earlier. When the emigrants reached America's east coast this ongoing westerly odyssey continued unabated across the vast continent with the billowing calico of canvas wagons replacing that of full filled sails. Teddy Roosevelt said that the Scots Irish were, "the Kernel of the distinctively and intensely American stock who were the pioneers of our people on their march westward". John Steinbeck wrote about the Hamiltons, his maternal Scots Irish ancestors 'westering' out to California.

3

The Struggle For Independence

"We have lost America through the Irish" – Lord Mountjoy - House of Commons.

"I hear that our American cousin has run off with a Scots Irish parson". Horace Walpole – British Prime Minister.

"Call this war whatever you may, only call it not an American rebellion: it is nothing more that a Scots Irish Presbyterian Rebellion" – British Officer writing in 1778.

The rough draft of the First Declaration of Independence was drawn up by Charles Thomson who was Secretary of the First Continental Congress. Charles Thomson was born on 29th November 1729 in Gorteade Cottage Upperlands Co Londonderry. His father decided to emigrate to America in 1739 but became sick and died on board ship within sight of landing at New Castle at the Head of the Delaware Bay. As a boy Thomson was fortunate to enter the Academy of Dr Francis Allison the renowned teacher of New London Pennsylvania. Within a few years Thomson himself was running his own school before he moved to Philadelphia where he became friendly with Benjamin Franklin. He became an organiser and an agitator for the cause of American Independence. In August 1774 he was elected Secretary of the First Continental Congress and he held this position until 1781 when he became Secretary of the United States in Congress which he remained until 1789.

On July 4th 1776 the original Declaration of Independence was signed by only two people – Charles Thomson as Secretary and John Hancock as President of the Continental Congress. The beautifully flowing prose of this document was almost entirely the work of Thomas Jefferson. John Hancock the other signature to this document was a Scot Irish man whose origins were in the Co Down town of Banbridge. The Scots Irish plot then thickens when we consider that they took the signed Declaration to John Dunlap a Philadelphia printer who printed 500 Hancock/Thomson 'typed signed' Broadsides which were distributed to the members of Congress and the King of England. The actual original signed document itself was lost in what has been described as, "the Fever of Freedom" which ensued after these events.

On August 2nd 1776 the delegates returned to Philadelphia to sign a newly prepared Declaration of Independence and for some reason Thomson was not invited to sign.

For fifteen years, from the outbreak of the Revolution to the ratification of the New Constitution, Congress met in Philadelphia and new laws were enacted and orders issued. The sessions always ended with the delegates returning to their respective States. Upon their departure one man was responsible for carrying on the business of the Government of the United States – Charles Thomson.

Among Thomson's other achievements was the creation of the design for the symbol of America; The Great Seal of the United States. The seal was adopted by the Continental

Congress on July 20th 1782. In the centre is the American eagle which holds in its beak a scroll inscribed – "E Pluribus Unum", in one talon is an olive branch, in the other a bundle of thirteen arrows. A shield with thirteen alternative red and white stripes covers the eagle's breast and over its head a cloud surrounds a blue field containing thirteen stars.

In 1808 he provided the first American translation from Greek of the oldest version of the Old Testament of the Bible and in the same year a translation of the New Testament. He died in Lower Merion, Montgomery County, Pennsylvania 16th August 1824.

Charles Thomson's brother William was taken to South Carolina by some members of the family and became famous for his skills with a rifle. He fought against the Regulators in 1771, became Sheriff of Orangeburg in 1772 and in 1775 Colonel of the 3rd South Carolina regiment known as the Rangers. He fought at Charleston in 1776 driving the English back from Sullivan's Island. He was taken prisoner after the capture of Charleston. He eventually became a member of the State Constitutional Convention and then an indigo – planter until 1786 when for the good of his declining health he visited Universal Springs Virginia where he died.

Mention was made earlier in this chapter of John Dunlap a native of Strabane, Co Tyrone as being he who first printed the Declaration of Independence. Dunlap is also remembered as having been the founder of the first daily newspaper in America – The Pennsylvania Packet.

The Declaration of Independence also had the fingerprints of other Ulstermen all over it and the later August 2nd 1776 version contained nine Scots Irish signatories amongst the fifty six people who signed it. These were William Whipple, James Smith, Robert Paine from Dungannon, Thomas McKean from Ballymoney, Thomas Nelson from Strabane, Matthew Thornton from Londonderry and who became President of New Hampshire provincial Assembly ironically representing Londonderry New Hampshire in that Assembly and John Hancock from Banbridge. The latter signature was written in huge letters because Hancock said he knew that George III was short sighted and he wanted him to be able to read it. Bearing in mind Horace Walpole's comments at the head of this chapter it is interesting to note that both George Taylor and Edward Rutledge were the sons of Ulster clergymen. Philip Livingstone who was a Scot also signed the declaration albeit his great grandfather was also a Co Down Presbyterian Minister. The slogan on that Great Seal designed by Charles Thomson "E Pluribus Unum," reinforced the notion that the Scots Irish pioneers had contributed hugely to the plurality out of which one single United States was created.

4

Francis Hutcheson

FRANCIS Hutcheson never actually visited America in person but his thoughts and philosophies did make the journey and had a huge impact on the framing of both the Declaration of Independence and on the Constitution of the United States of America.

Francis Hutcheson was born on August 8th 1694 at his grandfather's house at Drumalig, near Saintfield. This grandfather had travelled to the drumlins of County Down from Ayrshire to minister to the Scots who had settled in the area.

In the next generation Francis' father John was also a Presbyterian minister who was called to a congregation in Downpatrick before moving later to the city of Armagh.

It was here that young Francis spent his very early years.

Aged eight Francis returned to his grandfather's place in County Down and attended Mr John Hamilton's school, which was accommodated in a disused meeting house near Saintfield. Here the young Hutcheson was grounded in the classical languages which he was later to use so adeptly.

Francis Hutcheson

From here he transferred to Mr James McAlpin's 'philosophy school' in Killyleagh. A fellow pupil at this academy was his cousin James Bruce who was the son of William Bruce the local dissenter clergyman.

This school provided an alternative route for dissenters who were determined to make their way in the civic life of Ulster notwithstanding Church or Ireland predominance and restrictions.

The academy's courses were of a high standard and included studies in Logic, Metaphysics and Moral Philosophy.

Shortly after his grandfather's death in 1711 the subsequent financial inheritance allowed Francis to enrol as a student at Glasgow University in 1713.

The University staff at this time included a number of radical and unconventional academics. Particularly notable was Professor Stinson who was head of the faculty of Theology and espoused and expounded liberal theological opinions and beliefs.

Francis Hutcheson completed his studies here in 1717 and after a short period returned as a probationary minister to work with his father's congregation in Armagh.

On one particular Sunday Francis preached the sermon as a substitute for his father who was temporarily ill.

Historian Philip Orr tells us that one member of the Armagh congregation was moved to complain to Hutcheson senior that Francis had, "fashed a' the congregation wi' his idle cackle, for he was babbling this 'oor about the good and benevolent God and that the souls o' the heathen themsel's will gang to heaven, if they follow the licht o'their ain consciences. Not a word does the daft boy ken nor say aboot the gude auld comfortable doctrines o' election, reprobation, original sin and faith."

Notwithstanding the controversy that he sometimes provoked, or perhaps because of it, in 1720 Francis was 'called' to the Presbyterian congregation at Magherally, county Down.

However, this business of ministering to Presbyterians in Ulster was not how Hutcheson was to make his way in the world.

In the following year Hutcheson obtained a position running a private academy for the dissenting population of Dublin who had mostly settled there during the Cromwellian period.

Thomas Drennan who also taught at the school, was the father of Dr William Drennan, later to become a leading United Irishman and a particular favourite of Mary Ann McCracken. In Dublin Hutcheson mingled with a circle of free-thinkers and radical opinion-makers which included Lord Molesworth.

It was during this period that he wrote some of his most enduring and seminal works.

In the period from 1723 until 1725 Francis Hutcheson wrote and published 'An Enquiry into Beauty and Virtue' and by 1728 he had written and published 'Essays on the nature and conduct of the passions and affections with illustrations on the moral sense'.

This latter treatise argued that rather than emphasising the concept of 'original sin', it is 'love' and 'virtue' that are inherent in human beings.

Hutcheson's position was that not only were these faculties innate and inevitably demonstrated by people but also that doing so gave intense pleasure and 'happiness' to individuals.

Meanwhile Hutcheson's conservatively-minded father was becoming concerned at the unconventional company that Francis was keeping in Dublin and the Anglican establishment were affronted at his daring "to take upon himself the education of youth" so there was a sense of relief in more than one camp when in 1729 the thirty five year old Presbyterian preacher from Ulster was appointed as Professor of Moral Philosophy at his old university in Glasgow.

This proved to be a prescient move and within a very short period of time Hutcheson became one of the stars in a constellation that was known as 'The Scottish Enlightenment'.

Overall this movement – and Hutcheson as an integral part thereof – was to have a huge impact, particularly on the political history and constitution of the United States.

Hutcheson's work had both a direct and an indirect impact. Arguably and paradoxically it was the latter which was the more powerful force and had the most lasting effect on the creation of the United States of America.

The direct impact came through Hutcheson's writings. Bernard Bailyn in his publication '*Pamphlets of the American Revolution, 1756-1776*' tells us that Hutcheson was a figure that "the colonists know and cited" in the mid 18th century.

In particular he adds that although Hutcheson was himself a Presbyterian minister he was "for absolute freedom of conscience and of public religious exercise."

By an indirect route Hutcheson's teaching was to have an impact that was 'at arms length' , but was nothing short of seismic in its effect.

As a 17 year old Virginian of the wealthy class Thomas Jefferson came to attend William and Mary College in Williamsburg in his home state.

He walked through these elegant, classically designed doors in 1760, some 14 years after the death in Dublin of Francis Hutcheson.

Still very much alive however, and residing in America, were the burning ideals of Francis Hutcheson, now espoused by many of his former students turned teachers.

One such 'disciple' was Dr William Small who had recently arrived at the college from Scotland.

Small's teaching upheld the tenets of Hutcheson's central notions of 'liberty' and 'virtue'.

Jefferson said of Dr Small that he "probably fixed the destinies of my life".

Although Jefferson had been raised as an Anglican/Episcopalian he is considered by some to have become a 'deist' in adult life.

He relied on reason rather than revelation to shape his moral code. As far as Jefferson was concerned the moral issue was not whether God existed but rather that all views on the subject ought to be tolerated – "it does me no injury for my neighbour to say that there are twenty gods or no God. It neither picks my pocket nor breaks my leg."

Francis Hutcheson had written in his 1725 work about 'unalienable rights', which he saw as paramount and which controlled all governments and powers in how they dealt with individuals. This apparent truth spoke loudly and clearly to Thomas Jefferson and provided for him a sound justification for the American colonists to seek independence from Britain.

It is easy to see why he would have thought this way if examination is made of Hutcheson's actual words – "for whenever any invasion is made upon unalienable rights, there must arise either a perfect or extreme right to resistance... unalienable rights are essential limitations in all governments."

Not only do the words provide justification for the American Revolution but the phrase 'unalienable rights' taken with Hutcheson's reference to 'happiness' chimes clearly with Jefferson's concept of 'inalienable rights' and with the Declaration of Independence 'checklist' to which he appended "the pursuit of happiness" as an indispensable item.

Jefferson was the architect of the Declaration document which contained this element. However, he was not the designer of the actual American Constitution. This role was to fall to his friend James Madison.

Here again Hutcheson played his part through the work of a former student, for Dr Witherspoon was Madison's mentor in a similar way to Dr Small for Thomas Jefferson and this time Princeton provided the context rather than Virginia's William and Mary College.

Madison was much influenced by Witherspoon who was an advocate of the scientific method of testing any theory against experience.

He believed that freedom was crucial if education was to fulfil its function of broadening and deepening the mind and spirit.

Garry Wills tells us that "Hutcheson was the author of the central topic of philosophy as it was taught at Philadelphia and Princeton and New York. What was true elsewhere was doubly true of William and Mary in Dr Small's time there".

He has further explained that Thomas Jefferson had a very minimal role in formulating the Constitution since he was Minister to France from 1785-89.

It is clear that the Constitution was the work of James Madison, Alexander Hamilton and John Jay.

Wills explains this most clearly – "Madison under Witherspoon, like Jefferson under Small had shaped his politics to Scottish Enlightenment ways."

Amazing as it may seem, this aspect of Hutcheson's influence had even further effect. When the slave-owning Jefferson wrote that "all men are created equal", he was thinking only of male colonists without any consideration being given to his black or female peers. During his lifetime Hutcheson abhorred slavery and believed that freedom encompassed "all people".

Later in America history anti-slavery abolitionists would lock into 'unalienable rights' as would Elizabeth Cady Stanton when she promoted Women's Suffrage. Dr Martin Luther King used the philosophy of 'unalienable rights' to underpin the Civil Rights campaign.Hutcheson's relatively lowly background belies the mighty impact of his writing of what remain today as very revolutionary philosophies for life.

James Smith, Original Portrait

5

JAMES SMITH

ALTHOUGH several of the men who signed the Declaration of Independence were the sons or grandsons of emigrants from Ulster there were three signatures which belonged to men who were actually born in the Province. Their names were, James Smith, George Taylor and Matthew Thornton.

James Smith was born the second son of an Ulster Presbyterian family sometime around 1719. It is difficult to be more precise since Smith kept his age as a secret. When he was just a lad of around 10 years old, his father a much respected farmer, brought him to America. The family settled on the Susquehanna River in York County Pennsylvania. It was there that Mr Smith senior died in 1761. James Smith was a person of singular intellect from an early age. His father was determined that he would have a liberal education. So James was placed in school with the renowned and aforementioned Rev. Dr Allison who was provost of the college (or academy) of New London Pennsylvania. In this centre of learning James

James Smith Residence

Smith studied Latin, Greek and practical Surveying. Later he read law with his elder brother in the Lancaster Pennsylvania office of Thomas Cookson. On being admitted to the bar he took up a position as a lawyer and surveyor near the present day town of Shippensburg. After a period of time he moved to York and established himself there in his chosen profession.

At age 40 James Smith married Eleanor Armor, a girl from Newcastle Delaware, who was twenty years his junior. He owned and worked extensive iron manufacturing works on Coduras Creek and by the start of the American Revolution he was a man of considerable substance and property. Initially he was not all that interested in politics and it was only after 'The Boston Tea Party' when Parliament closed the port as punishment that he decided to become involved in the American patriot cause. James Smith was viewed by his contemporaries as being something of a wit with an eccentric persona. One of his neighbours said, "He loved wine, and drank much of it."

At the outbreak of hostilities with Great Britain James Smith embraced the American cause with fervour. He was a delegate from York County to a meeting of all the Pennsylvania counties which was held in 1774. This meeting culminated in a decision to abstain from importing any goods from England. Shortly after his return to York James Smith raised a corps of volunteers. This was the first such body raised in Pennsylvania

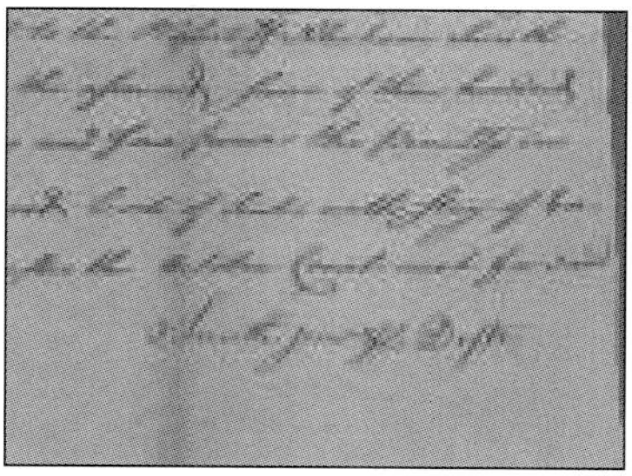

James Smith, Signer and Signature

in opposition to Great Britain. Smith was elected as Captain of this corps/company and when it eventually grew to be a regiment he was appointed Colonel. In his case this was an honorary title since he never physically assumed command.

In January 1775 a convention for the Province of Pennsylvania was assembled. Smith was a member of same and supported the strong anti-British line that was drawn at this event.

On the 15th of May of that same year Congress adopted a resolution that in all but name declared independence. A plan was adopted to assemble a provincial conference for the purpose of forming a new government.

The conference assembled on June 18th and Smith was prominent as an engaging and distinguished speaker who held strong views on the matter. A unanimous decision was taken there to issue a Declaration of Independence. This was presented to Congress exactly one week later and provided the core of the Declaration which was eventually pronounced.

One month later in July a convention assembled in Philadelphia for the purpose of forming a new constitution for Pennsylvania. Colonel Smith was elected as a member of this body and took his seat on 15 July. Five days later he was elected by the Convention to Congress. Thereafter Smith became a promoter and early propagandist for American Independence.

On the evening of July 6th 1776 Continental army Captain Francis Wade of Delaware and a Dr Young accompanied Smith to Yorktown. They had travelled from bustling Philadelphia to try to garner the public's reaction to the reading of a copy of the Declaration of Independence. The diarist of York County, John Adlum later wrote, "I do not believe that the majority, men and women, knew what independence meant".

In Yorktown on that July evening a crowd of 300-400 people had assembled. Wade and Young made short speeches and read from the Declaration of Independence. However Smith's speech was the one that caught the public imagination. It brimmed with fervour and enthusiasm, at a time when people knew little of the detail of what was proposed. He outlined all the benefits of independence and literally threw his hat in the air whilst cheering for liberty. Those gathered were caught up by his oratory and showed their support by likewise throwing their hats in the air.

James Smith remained an efficient and active member of Congress for a number of years. He withdrew from the House in November 1778 and returned to his original profession as a lawyer. In 1800 he finally withdrew from the bar which he had graced for 60 years. He died in York in 1806 and was survived by two of his five children. He was buried there in the 1st Presbyterian Church. James Smith was remembered as a man who loved anecdotes, and conviviality. It is believed that he was aged 87 when he died but no one knows for certain as he kept his age a secret. He will be remembered by Americans for the certainty that he brought to the 'Patriot Cause'.

George Taylor

6

A Portrait of George Taylor

George Taylor led a life that was very mobile and both publicly and personally controversial.

He was born in Ulster in 1716, though we are not sure as to exactly where his birthplace might have been.

There is some suggestion that it may have been Belfast but nothing has been proven in this regard.

It is known that Taylor's father was a clergyman although the exact denomination of this calling is also not known. In the United States George Taylor worshipped as a Presbyterian. In his late teens in Ulster he began to study medicine but relinquished this course of action shortly before he set sail for America as an 'indentured servant' in 1736.

In order to pay for his passage George Taylor took a job as an iron-worker and then as a clerk at the Warwick Iron Furnace in Coventry, Chester County, Pennsylvania. By 1739 he had become manager of a plantation of 1,796 acres. In 1742 he married Anne Savage who was the widow of the ironmaster for

George Taylor Residence

whom he had been working. By 1747 he had distinguished himself as a Captain in Benjamin Franklin's volunteer private militia force which had been commissioned to protect the colony from frontier violence. In this capacity he gained a reputation as one who supported the radical cause of the 'ordinary citizen' – the artisan, the small merchant, the labourer and farm worker. In the mid 1750's George Taylor moved in to Bucks County where he leased Durham Furnace near the city of Easton. In 1768 his wife died and thereafter over the years Taylor had five children out of wedlock by his housekeeper. In all this time Taylor remained fiercely independent and within the Provincial Assembly held on to his opposition to the concept of a 'Royal Government'. This was a plan that had been proposed at the time by no less a personage than Benjamin Franklin himself. In the following year George Taylor served on a committee that wrote the instructions for Pennsylvania's delegates to the Stamp Act Congress. In this respect he worked with other delegates to ensure increased representation for the back country.

George Taylor House

George Taylor Marker

From 1769 – 70 George Taylor was a member of the Pennsylvania Assembly and in July 1775 he was elected to the position of Colonel of Bucks County Assembly. He was sent from there to the Pennsylvania Assembly in October 1775 and he served this body with distinction, on several important committees, particularly that which drafted instructions to the delegates to the Continental Congress in November of that year.

One year later on July 20th 1776 Taylor was appointed to the Continental Congress with four other delegates to replace those Pennsylvanian delegates who had refused to sign the Declaration of Independence. He signed the 'engrossed copy' of August 2nd but took little other part in the activities of Congress. In March 1777 he was elected from Northampton County to the new Supreme Executive Council of Pennsylvania

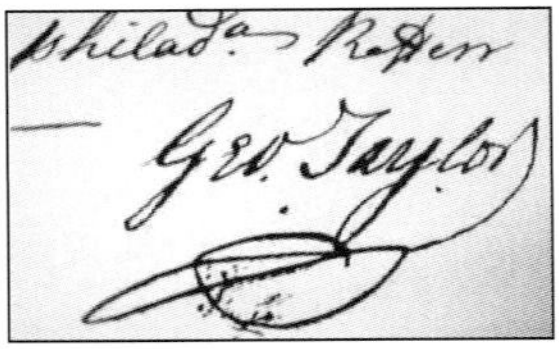

Signature

but because of illness was only able to serve for six weeks before retiring from public affairs.

During the years 1775 - 1778 George Taylor was very involved in the practical production of ordnance and ammunition for the Revolutionary War effort. He leased the Durham Furnace in Pennsylvania and produced such items as grape shot, cannon balls, bar shot and actual cannon. In 1778 Taylor was dispossessed from ownership of these works by the well-known Philadelphia loyalist – John Galloway who owned the furnace and who had fled to New York in 1776. Taylor then leased the forge in the New Jersey town of Greenwich and continued his 'war effort' operations for three further years. In April 1780 he moved to Easton Pennsylvania where he died in 1781 aged 65. He was originally interred in the German Evangelical churchyard in Easton but sometime thereafter his body was moved to the main Easton cemetery. George Taylor, who had been at the centre of the ferment both strategically and practically passed away without ever knowing how the American Revolution had turned out.

7

MATTHEW THORNTON

MATTHEW Thornton was born in Ulster in 1714. When he was three years of age his father James decided to emigrate to America. The Thornton family settled first outside Brunswick Maine on a plot of land overlooking Maquoit Bay on Rossmore Road. In 1976 the Brunswick Knights of Columbus placed a granite marker on the site of the former Thornton homestead.

Often accounts of Thornton's life state that the family settled at 'Wiscasset Maine', but this is not correct. In and around 1720 Brunswick was the outpost of the "Eastern territory" and was on the frontline that stood between the aspirations and momentum of three major cultures, each of which was seeking its own territory.

This triangle of struggle consisted of:-

The English in Boston and Falmouth to the West.

The Native American peoples to the North and in the interior.

Matthew Thornton

The French of Acadia, Nova Scotia and the St. Lawrence to the East.

In a way this juxtaposition was prophetic - for Matthew Thornton's private and public life was to engage at different times, with the struggles of all three contenders.

The first such encounter was to occur five years later; on July 11th 1722 when a band of Native Americans attacked the town. James Thornton, his wife Elizabeth and their young son Matthew fled from their burning home and escaped by canoe. Narrowly escaping death they made their way initially to Casco Bay Maine. From there they moved to the Scots Irish settlement of Worcester Massachusetts. In Worcester Matthew Thornton received a classical education at the Worcester Academy. The family subsequently left Worcester as a result of the bad treatment meted out to the Scots Irish of the town by the Congregationalist Puritan burghers. Matthew Thornton completed his studies in Medicine in Leicester and then in 1740 opened up his medical practice in Londonderry New Hampshire. This proved to be a position which was financially lucrative and Thornton became a wealthy citizen. Londonderry was relatively small at this time but by 1775 it had grown to become the second largest town in New Hampshire in both population and taxable wealth.

In 1745, five years after he had hung out his Doctor's slate in Londonderry, Matthew Thornton was still a bachelor and decided to volunteer his services as a military surgeon on the 'Fort Louisburg' expedition to Cape Breton. This was a major British campaign against the French and ended with the taking of the aforementioned French fort at the mouth of the St Lawrence waterway.

During this campaign Matthew Thornton's skill as a surgeon was particularly noted. In spite of the magnitude of the operation, consequent from the fighting only 6 lives were lost on the British side. After this 'tour of duty' Matthew Thornton returned home to Londonderry New Hampshire where he remained in the local militia and eventually in 1775 received a commission as a Colonel from Governor Wentworth. Realistically however at 61 he was too old for active service. We have descriptions of Dr Matthew Thornton in the 1750's which portray him as tall, clear-eyed and handsome and added to this possessing a charm and storytelling capability that kept his friends enthralled for hours on end.

Matthew Thornton was 46 years of age when he married Hannah Jack in 1760 and the couple were to have five children. From the outset Thornton took an active part in the overthrow of the British governance in New Hampshire and was prominent in his opposition to the Stamp Act. In 1768 Matthew Thornton and the other members of his family were granted the township which still bears his name – Thornton.

In 1775 Matthew Thornton was elected President of the Convention and over the next decade held a series of positions as Chairman of committees and President of the Constitutional Convention.

Subsequently he became President of the fifth Congress which adopted the first Constitution of the Colonies on January 5th 1776. He also chaired the 5 man committee which drafted the document.

Although not elected until November 4th 1776 and thus after the passage of the Declaration of Independence, Matthew Thornton was allowed to sign the engrossed copy of the document. He had attested and it had been fully accepted that retrospectively he was fully in accordance with the voting on the issue. Thornton arrived in Philadelphia just one day before he signed the Declaration and commenced his two year stint in Congress. Some 18 months prior to his arrival in Philadelphia Matthew Thornton had written a letter to Congress advocating complete independence from Great Britain. This was a view that was not universally supported at the time. However by November 1776 it was the almost unanimous viewpoint of the activists in the Colonies.

After the adoption of the January 1776 Constitution, the first in the Colonies, Thornton was elected as the first speaker of the House. Subsequently he became a member of the Council although Meslech Weare was named as Head of this Body.

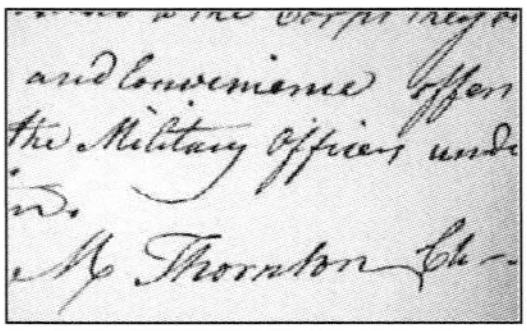

Signature

Matthew Thornton in later years

From 1776 until 1782 Matthew Thornton served as Chief Justice of the Court of Common Pleas – the superior court of New Hampshire. In 1779 he returned to Exeter New Hampshire and in 1780 settled his family there on a farm which he purchased when it was confiscated from the prominent Tory – Edward Goldstone Lutwyche. As part of this land in Merrimack County he owned a ferry on the Merrimack River which is known to this day as Thornton's ferry. He gave up his medical practice at this time.

In his 70's from 1784 – 1787 Matthew Thornton was a member of the New Hampshire State Senate and coupled this with an adjunct role from 1785 – 1786 as a State Councillor. Double tragedy struck him within a twelve month period when in 1786 his wife died and his son passed away the following year. Thornton himself had increasing infirmities and shortly

Matthew Thornton Headstone

Matthew Thornton Home

Matthew Thornton Marker

after this he retired from public life. Nonetheless he continued to write articles on matters of the day throughout his eighties. In his last days he composed but didn't publish a metaphysical work on the origin of sin.

Matthew Thornton died on June 24th 1803 aged 89 whilst on a visit to the home of his daughter in Newburyport Massachusetts.

In 1887 the legislature of New Hampshire voted $1000 for a monument to be placed over Matthew Thornton's grave in Merrimack New Hampshire. Other monuments and memorials were to follow including that which gave his name to the 'Matthew Thornton High School' in Londonderry New Hampshire. He will be especially remembered here in Ulster for the fact that during the period of transition of the American Legislature from the British to the Provincial authorities, Matthew Thornton, an Ulsterman by birth, was viewed by many as the leader of the Government.

8

The Patriot Mitchell Family of Elkton, Maryland

THE family of Revolutionary War patriot Dr Abraham David Mitchell was decidedly Scots Irish. Like many Ulster emigrants his father's family initially settled in Lancaster County Pennsylvania. However at age 25 Abraham moved to settle a short distance across the Mason Dixon line in Cecil County Maryland.

Dr Abraham Mitchell lived at the family home of Fair Hill Maryland which today is an international centre for equestrian events. He also designed and built a house on Main Street Elkton which he converted into a hospital where her personally treated hundreds of American soldiers during the Revolutionary War against the British. During this time the Marquis de Lafayette, who was a friend of Abraham Mitchell's son George, visited the Elkton home/hospital. This event is commemorated with an historical marker on the site.

Dr Abraham Mitchell was one of the most distinguished physicians of his time and his practice extended over the greater part of Cecil County Maryland. At this time his cousin Rev. Alexander Mitchell was prominent as Presbyterian Minister at Octoraro and Doe Run Churches in Chester County Pennsylvania. During the latter part of his life Dr Mitchell was a member of the famous Rock Presbyterian Church. He died at Fair Hill on 30th September 1817 in his 84th year.

Dr Abraham Mitchell's aforementioned son George also studied medicine, initially under his father's tutelage. After attending the Medical Department of the University of Pennsylvania he went into partnership in his father's medical practice in Elkton. In 1806 he was elected to a seat in the General Assembly of Maryland. For his distinguished service in the war of 1812 he was breveted as a Colonel in the regular army. He resigned his commission in 1821 and returned to Fair Hill where he was very involved in agricultural pursuits. In the fall of 1822 he was elected a member of the 18th Congress as a Democrat to represent the Congressional District of Cecil, Kent and Harford Counties Maryland.

Dr George Mitchell's brother Ephraim Thompson Mitchell was born in 1783 and having studied for the legal profession ultimately gave his life in the war against the British. He died

The Mitchell Home, Fair Hill, Maryland

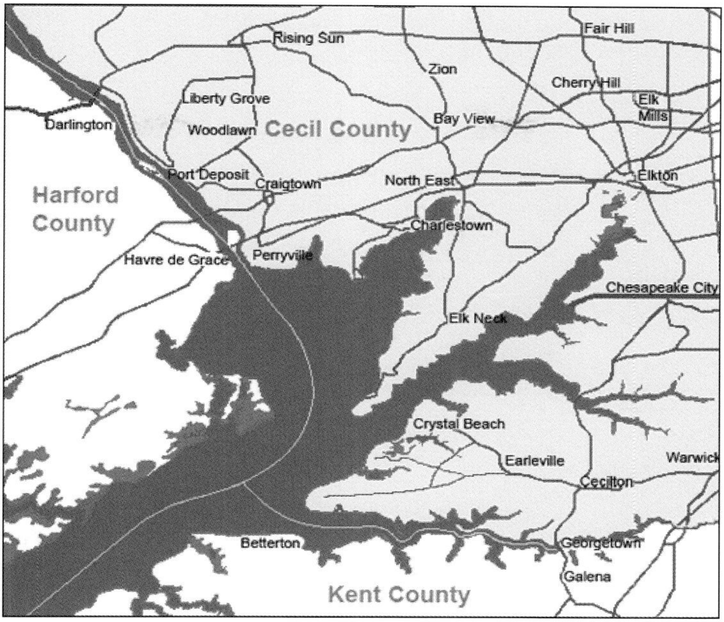

Elkton, Maryland

whilst on board The Lady Provost on Lake Erie en route from Detroit to Fort George.

Another brother born in 1786 named Abraham David after his father the patriarch of the family, married Jane Thompson Evans whose maternal great-grandmother Janet Creigh was born in Carnmoney Co. Antrim in 1716 and as a widow with two children emigrated from Belfast to Pennsylvania in 1761. The Creighs also gave outstanding service in the Revolutionary War and Jane Evans' grandfather John Creigh (born Carnmoney 1741) served as a Lieutenant Colonel at Perth Amboy in 1776.

Today the Mitchell houses at both Elkton and Fair Hill are listed on the National Register of Historic Places in America and a plaque in Valley Forge Memorial Chapel honours the memory of Dr Abraham Mitchell who was both a great Ulster Scot and a noble American patriot.

The Mitchell Family Home, Elkton

9

Entrepreneurs

CONSIDER the lives of three Scots Irish entrepreneurs who contributed much to the emergence of the North American continent – John Macomb, Alexander Turney Stewart and Timothy Eaton, and certain trends emerge in terms of that which is common in their biographies.

For two out of the three New York was important as a base for their business; for another two out of the three the building and development of Department Stores was important; another two out of the three established family business dynasties. Of course it was not the same two out of the three each time because, as is the way of things, their life-stories overlapped each other. All three showed the Scots Irish characteristics of courage, innovation and a willingness to take on fresh challenges in fresh fields. All three became millionaires.

Here is their story:-

JOHN GORDON MACOMB made his fortune by procuring and supplying the particular needs of the wealthy market that a standing army represents. His family were Scots

Irish of three generations standing, who settled in Ulster in 1619 at the Scots colony of Donegore in Co Antrim. Almost a century later when John Gordon Macomb was born, in 1717, they had moved a short distance within Co Antrim to Dunturkey near Ballyclare.

John Gordon Macomb was by no means poor, being already a successful businessman with premises in Bridge Street Belfast – near the docks - as is then was, when he decided to emigrate to America in 1755. He sailed with his wife Jane, sons William and Alexander and daughter Anne. John Macomb saw the potential of developing his mercantile career further by supplying the luxury needs of officers in the British Colonial Army. Either he possessed considerable luck or he had considerable foresight in this decision in that the army did not receive formal orders to move to America in significant numbers until a couple of years later with the onset of the seven year French and Indian war.

Call it what you will – intuition had led Macomb to establish his business base in Albany New York. From there he supplied officers with all manner of fancy goods from telescopes and books to snuff and wine. By the end of the Seven Year War Macomb had prospered sufficiently to be appointed as a County Judge.

In 1775 the American Colonies declared Independence and Macomb's foresight and good fortune faltered in that he backed the losing British forces instrumentally by himself supplying five hundred men to support General Burgoyne at the Battle of Bennington. This caused him to have a narrow escape when he was hunted like a fox through the woodlands of New York State. He narrowly escaped with his life.

The Macomb entrepreneurial dynasty was built further however by his son Alexander who was only seven when he left Dunturkey. Eleven years later he, like his father before, him struck out for fresh challenges when he left New York and headed west for Detroit Michigan, which was then on the frontier of the wilderness. Here he developed a lucrative business in bartering for furs with the Indians. By the time Alexander Macomb had reached 26 years of age his business accounted for one third of the entire fur trade of North America. During the War of Independence, unlike his father and brother William, Alexander Macomb supported the American cause and was in favour to such an extent that he was able to buy from the American Government 4.5 million acres of land – in fact much of the State of New York. This deal became known as 'Macomb's Purchase'. He owned a house at 39 Broadway in New York City which he loaned to George Washington who made it his temporary residence in 1790, when Washington was ill and convalesced there in the period when New York was 'capital' of the emerging republic that would grow into the United States. Alexander Macomb senior died in Georgetown DC in 1831. His son also called Alexander was born in Detroit 3rd April 1782 and received a classical education in Newark New Jersey. In time he was to join the American army and fulfil the ultimate goal for a soldier when he was appointed Major General and Commander-in-Chief of the American army. This was a post which he held from 1828 until 1841. Many soldiers across America returning from the war of 1812 had named towns and counties 'Macomb' in honour of their hero.

The Macomb family's entrepreneurial history represents a microcosm of the colonial business history of America. The family moved from supplying British troops to commanding the American forces. In all their enterprises they looked for the opportunity to 'read the runes' of supply and demand in America and to strike out for new challenges and new markets whilst pushing the frontier back in more ways than one.

ALEXANDER TURNEY STEWART also began his fantastic entrepreneurial career in New York. Of all the Americans who have figured in 'America's Richest' Register Alexander Turney Stewart is today still listed as the 5th richest American of all time. When he died in 1876 the whole front page of the New York Times was filled with the details of his funeral and the names of the legions of prominent American citizens who attended the ceremony to pay homage to his memory and achievements.

In contrast with this recognition Turney Stewart's was a life that had begun very inauspiciously 73 years earlier when he was born on a tenant farm at Knocknaree in the townland of Lissue near Lisburn. Alexander's father died shortly after he was born and his young mother remarried almost immediately. Shortly after her wedding she and her new husband emigrated to New York. However Alexander's maternal grandfather – Turney was not comfortable with the baby accompanying his mother and stepfather at this time and kept the boy at Lissue until he was well into his teenage years. Ironically his mother's choice of New York as her new home gave Stewart an almost accidental connection with the city where he would eventually make his fortune. Having received a classical education in nearby Magheragall and spent much of his time amongst his Ulster Quaker neighbours (where he absorbed their business patterns and beliefs) young Stewart initially became an apprentice in a store in Chichester Street Belfast. Always restless in this environment he set sail for New York when he was 17 years of age and initially worked for a brief time as a teacher.

When he had 'surveyed the lie of the land' in this way he returned home briefly and claimed his inheritance of approximately $10,000 from his grandfather Turney. With this he developed a dry goods business and in time opened the first Department store in the world which New Yorkers dubbed the

'Great Iron Store'. This was eventually sold as Wannamaker's and is today the site of Macy's New York landmark store. By 1848 Stewart had become a millionaire and when he developed an even bigger, grander store the 'Hawkeye novelist' James Fenimore Cooper described it as being "more like a palace than a store". This phrase struck a note with the public and it became known simply as, 'The Marble Palace'. In time Stewart opened branches of his business empire in Paris, Belfast, Chicago, London and Philadelphia and diversified into owning hotels and theatres.

During the American Civil War Stewart supported the Northern cause and donated more than $5,000,000 in equipping Lincoln's Union Army. After the war when President Lincoln mooted the notion of repaying Stewart for his contribution he casually dismissed the matter with a scratch of his pen saying, "Don't mention it – it was nothing".

The Civil War also affected his beloved Ulster however in that the "Cotton Famine" impacted in particular on the Lagan Valley since the supplies of cotton from the Confederate States were severely disrupted. Turney Stewart sent a ship to Belfast Lough which was loaded with grain for the relief of the suffering of the poor cotton weavers of the rural areas around his native Lisburn. On the return journey in place of the offloaded cargo, he took 139 emigrants from the area and gave these friends and former neighbours jobs in his thriving business enterprises in New York.

Notwithstanding his all time position, in his own lifetime he became the third wealthiest living American just behind William Astor and Cornelius Vanderbilt. Both these Millionaires had built their fortunes as a result of the efforts of more than one generation of family dynasties. In Stewart's case he was a 'self-made man' and exhibited the traits of risk taking, self-confidence and foresight that became the recurring characteristics of the Scots Irish in their business ventures in America and throughout the world.

In 1869 he put these skills to good use when he designed, developed and built Garden City on Long Island New York. He established no dynasty however for he and his wife Cornelia had no children of their own. Turney Stewart's wealth was renowned in his own era to such an extent that shortly after his death in 1876 there followed a bizarre incident in which his body was 'kidnapped' and held to ransom before being eventually returned for burial in the crypt of Garden City Cathedral.

He was an entrepreneur who, in one lifetime, achieved a momentous amount and had a tremendous impact on the business life of the United States in time of both war and peace.

In terms of the North America continent **TIMOTHY EATON** did for the Department Store in Canada a similar job to that which Alexander Turney Stewart had already carried out in the United States. Eaton's unique contribution, building on innovation, was his genius in combining the Department store with the development and popularising of the mail-order catalogue. With this he was able to supply shoppers across the vast prairies, mountains and wastelands of rural Canada. Like Turney Stewart he had come a long way from his roots in rural Ulster. Eaton was born in 1834 into a strict Presbyterian family on a farm near Ballymena. His older brothers and sisters had emigrated before him to Canada, their need to do so having been accentuated by the ravages of the Potato Famine in the area in 1846. Timothy Eaton decided that school was not for him and instead he was apprenticed to a small shop in nearby Portglenone for seven years. During this time it is reputed that he slept each night under the counter which he worked at during the day. Aged twenty he decided to venture forth and joined his brothers and sisters in Canada in 1854.

In 1856 the Eaton family opened a modest store in Kirkton and then later in St Mary's Ontario where they also ran a bakery. Timothy Eaton initially worked in these family businesses but in 1869 he struck out from the rest of the family and moved to Toronto which by then had amassed a population of seventy thousand citizens. He reckoned correctly that this offered him considerable market potential amongst an emerging industrial working class who had discovered newly found purchasing power. He opened a Department Store on Yonge Street where he was innovative in introducing 'fair deal' concepts that we now take for granted such as cash sales, fixed prices and refunds for unsatisfactory goods. Business prospered and in 1883 he built a bigger store with electric lighting and a fire safety sprinkler system. The store now stocked dry goods, clothing, hardware and electrical goods. However Eaton's entrepreneurial master-stroke came in 1884 with the introduction of his mail-order catalogue which was afterwards much deployed throughout both Europe and North America. At the time the concept was as revolutionary as is selling goods on the Internet today. The 'book' was known colloquially as the 'Farmers' Bible' and sold everything from kitchen gadgets to milking machines. Its advertising slogan claimed that it covered Canada from 'sea to sea' and meant that people living in remote areas now had access to goods that had previously been beyond their reach. So successful was the enterprise that a separate building had to be erected in Toronto as a warehouse for the mail-order business on its own.

In a more profound way than the other two Scots Irish entrepreneurs described here Eaton developed a reputation for being a humane employer. He introduced store closing and earlier staff 'quitting' at 6.00pm on weekdays and 2.00pm on Saturdays in July and August. He saw the ethical and practical benefits of allowing his staff time for relaxation and family recreation. By the time Eaton died in 1907 his was an entrepreneurial career that had seen the building of a second Department store in Winnipeg, two factories for the manufacture of 'own brand', goods, offices in Europe and the creation of an 'empire' that employed an overall work force of 9,000 people. Eaton's strict Reformed Faith remained a strong personality factor all his life and he resolutely refused to sell either liquor or tobacco. In memory of this aspect of his life and its impact on his business principles his family built and endowed the Timothy Eaton Memorial Church which opened in his beloved Toronto in 1913 where it is still thriving today.

As a result of his entrepreneurial flair Timothy Eaton's was a life that touched most, if not all, Canadians of his time and as a result of moving ahead of the times revolutionised shopping and business throughout the North American continent

10

THE PATTENS OF BATH MAINE - A SCOTS IRISH SEAGOING DYNASTY

IN the 1720's four Patten brothers emigrated from the City of Londonderry to Boston Massachusetts. A decade later the eldest of the brothers – Matthew travelled north of Boston to the Saco district of Maine where the land was plentiful and inexpensive. In 1738 two of his brothers – Actor (Hector) and Robert joined him in Saco. The fourth brother William stayed in Boston where be became a successful merchant.

In the early 18th century the district of Maine as it was termed was then part of Massachusetts and was truly the frontier, "between aggressive British empire builders and the defensive reactive French". The Native Americans were caught in the middle and took sides according to that which best served their own personal interests – sometimes one way, sometimes the other. Families such as the Pattens lived in constant fear of attack and loss of property. Not until 1763 when the British defeated the French and their 'Indian' allies did the region become safe and secure. In 1775 when the American

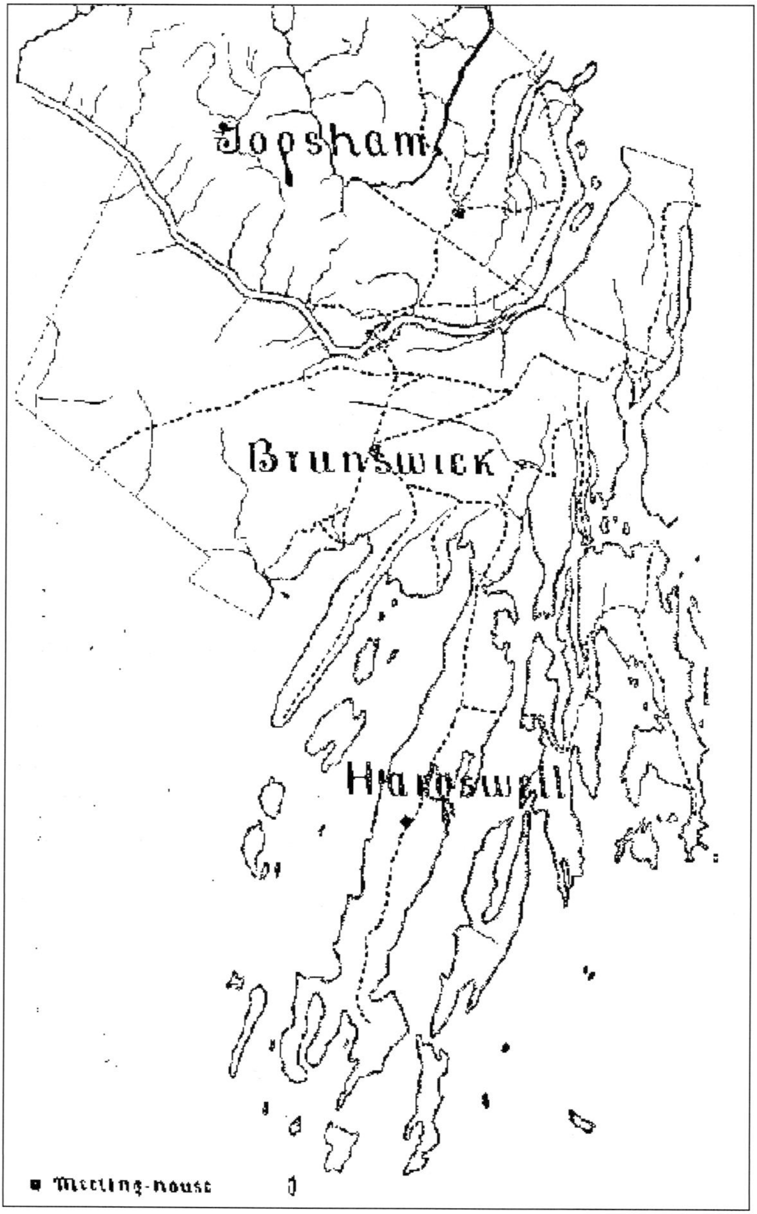

1764 Roads in Maine

Bath Maine Dock

Revolution erupted the settlers of Maine including the Pattens faced considerable difficulty because neither the Boston authorities nor the Continental Congress were in a strong enough position to be able to defend them. Many settlers left the area and others didn't live to see their pioneering efforts bear fruit. The Pattens stayed and were able to make a real success of their lives in Maine. Their initial occupation was farming but soon they were able to exploit the region's rich timber resources (Maine remains to this day the most wooded State in the Union) and tidal streams in two interlinked ways – (i) building small

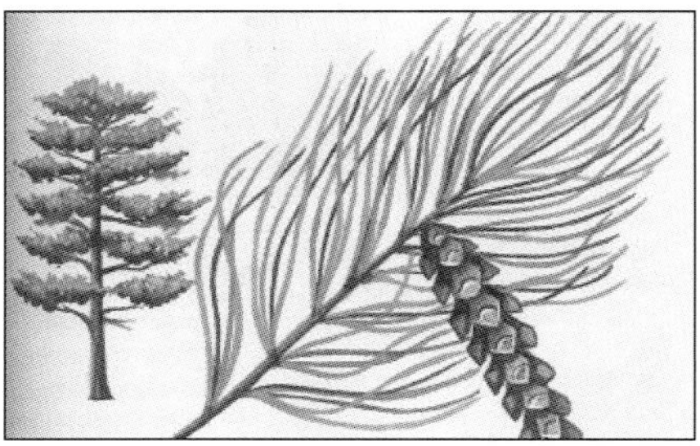

Maine White Pine

sailing vessels and (ii) drawing lumber and firewood to Boston and other ports along the coast.

The Pattens began a seafaring tradition there in Maine at the end of the eighteen century. The earliest records of the family show one of Matthew's sons – John as a captain of homebuilt vessels and eventually dying in a shipwreck in 1783. Another son Robert who continued to live in the Saco region is described as a Mariner and a shipbuilder right up until the time of his death in 1819 and we know that this branch of the family continued in shipbuilding for another generation.

Meanwhile Actor Patten moved east of Penobscot Bay to Surry with a group of Saco residents who found the confines of approaching civilization too restrictive. He died there during the American Revolution when the British were still in control of the region.

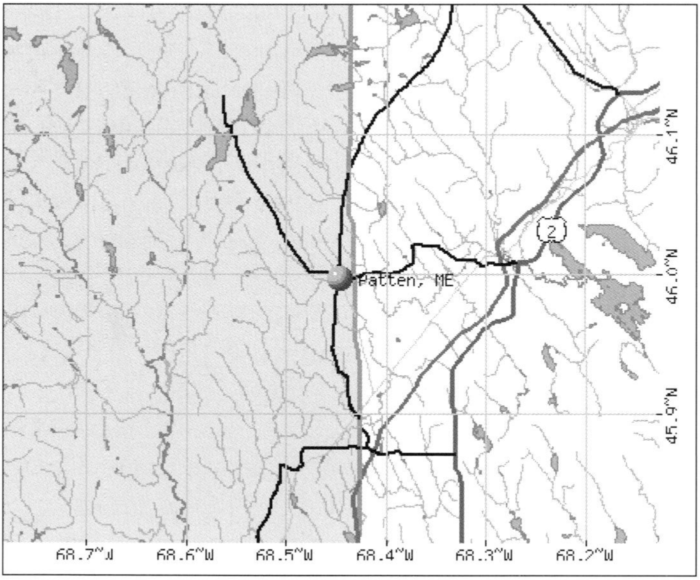

Patten, Maine

Patten, Maine

The true progenitor of the Patten maritime clan was Actor's son John who had been born in Ulster and accompanied his parents to America at age 10 and then moved to Saco with them. In 1749 John moved to the Topsham/Bowdoinham area of Maine and purchased there the rights to 661 acres on Cathance Point near Merrymeeting Bay. This is a broad tidal bay formed by the confluence of the Androscoggin, Cathance, Muddy, Abagadasset, Eastern and Kennebec rivers. As such it provided an ideal spot for shipbuilding given the potential to build ships with plenty of space and the ability to penetrate into the State of Maine in terms of timber and other produce. John cleared the land with the help of his brother William and his wife Mary's brother Thomas Means who also came from a prominent Maine Scots Irish family. John and Mary had 14 children. At one particularly favourable site within this land holding of John Patten's the city of Bath began to grow and prosper.

Early Maine historians George and Henry Wheeler have described the pioneer John Patten in this way, "a farmer (who) had also the trade of a blacksmith .... He also engaged in the lumber business ..., and was a proprietor in the Cathance Mill ... and of one – sixteenth of the saw mill and stream. He was somewhat engaged, also, in shipbuilding and navigation, and he, with John Fulton, Adam Hunter, and William Patten, built the first vessel ever launched above the 'chops' and the second built upon the Kennebec, above Bath."

The first vessel was launched in 1768 and was a 90 ton coasting sloop called the 'Merrymeeting'. The launch was a big event in the Cathance backwater. Most of John Patten's adult male neighbours were engaged in building the ship and the launch was an extended family Scots Irish affair with the Pattens providing dinner for all. William Patten the Merrymeeting's skipper loaded the ship with firewood which he sold in Boston on favourable terms and he also carried timber on subsequent voyages.

Another sloop 'Defiance' was built soon after and in 1772 John Patten and his partners launched the schooner 'Industry' which was the region's first vessel designed for the West Indies trade. This was extremely lucrative and locally sawn boards, shingles and masts fetched huge prices in the Caribbean. On the return journey the ship brought back rum, molasses and sugar which were in great demand. The American Revolution interrupted this trade however and the British forces harassed the citizens of the Maine coast - including the Patten family.

In August 1775 a party of Cathance farmers including John Patten's sons John and William and his son-in-law Robert Fulton set off on a 'haying' expedition. British forces captured them and took them to British territory – probable Nova Scotia. They were imprisoned and William Patten and Robert Fulton died during their incarceration. The rest were eventually set free but young John died shortly after his homecoming in 1780. This was a blow to the little tightly knit Scots Irish community along the Cathance shores.

Trade patterns shifted away from the Caribbean and in November 1824 the 'Catherine' set out on her maiden voyage carrying pine boards and shooks to Cuba. In January 1825 the same ship was on the way back from Havana and stopped to

Patten-built ship at Patten Point, Cathance River

load on cotton in New Orleans before proceeding to Liverpool where she arrived in April. Interestingly the ship arrived back from the British Isles to New York on 17th May 1825 loaded with emigrant passengers from Londonderry. Thereafter the increase in ship's tonnage was calibrated in the ships built to match the rise of the cotton trade. By 1839 the fleet consisted of a schooner, a brig and six ships – 'Cotton was King'.

The family succeeded as a result of timing, a 'tribal' spirit of cooperation, and as a result of having fire in their belly. They

Patten Free Library

Patten Library, Maine

were anxious to be seen as being successful as their sense of public charity and civic leadership later demonstrated. This included the building of the Patten Free Public Library in Bath Maine.

In 1913 Frank Patten, the last of the seagoing dynasty, retired from shipbuilding in Bath and moved to South Byfield Massachusetts where he started a chicken farm. He died of a severe cold within weeks of making the move.

Alister greets Bill McKeen at the Leach Library, Londonderry, N.H. Bill McKeen, President of the Maine Branch of St. Andrew's Society of America.

Saving and Sharing Maine's Scots-Irish Heritage

MAINE ULSTER SCOTS PROJECT

www.maineulsterscots.com

The Maine Ulster Scots Project (MUSP) has been created to promote awareness of Maine's Scots-Irish heritage and to gather and archive the histories of Maine's Ulster-Scots families, up to and including the time of the American Revolution. This history has been greatly overlooked and under-reported in many Maine history reference books.

They came here to make their own way, on their own terms.
They were not universally welcomed.

The following article is provided to us by Alister J. McReynolds who has made two trips to Maine to study the connections between the province of Ulster and the people of Maine, New England and Nova Scotia. The Maine Ulster Scots Project was pleased to host Mr. McReynolds during his trips here and were fortunate to have his expert guiding services this past August during a trip to Northern Ireland.
John T. Mann, Chair Maine Ulster Scots Project

Alister McReynolds is an Honorary Fellow of the University of Ulster, Institute of Ulster Scots Studies.

Introduction to an article by Alister which appeared in the 'Pine Tree Highlander'.

Alister McReynolds with Casey Cagle and Bernard Gilliland

Hear ye, Hear ye...

LISBURN writer and lecturer Alister McReynolds was in Atlanta recently and received a proclamation from Casey Cagle, the Lieutenant Governor of Georgia USA. The scroll declares May as 'Scots Irish' month in the State of Georgia. Also present was prominent Atlanta businessman and Scots Irish writer Bernard Gilliland.

Mr McReynolds is currently engaged in planning a joint Conference for next May on behalf of The University of Ulster Institute of Ulster Scots Studies, where he is an Honorary Research Fellow, and Georgia Southern University.

The conference will take place over a number of days in Savannah, Georgia.

Mr McReynolds is no stranger to Georgia having been the Keynote Speaker there this year at The American Conference for Irish Studies which was attended by delegates from over 55 North American, Irish and British universities.

Newspaper cutting from the Ulster Star.

Alister with Bernard Gillialand and Lieutenant Governor of Georgia, Casey Cagle.

Alister at Aghaloo old church, Co. Tyrone.

L-R: George Patton, Chief Executive Ulster Scots Agency, Eileen McReynolds, Alister McReynolds, Val Mann and John Mann displaying the flag of Maine which was flown over the State capital building on 'Scots Irish Day'.

Gravestone of John Patten and Hector (Actor) Patten.

Center for Irish Studies
Ionad an Léinn Éireannaigh
An Integral Part of the Georgia Southern Advantage

P.O. Box 8023
Georgia Southern University
Statesboro, GA 30460
Phone: (912) 681-5899
Fax: (912) 681-0653
irish@georgiasouthern.edu
http://class.georgiasouthern.edu/irish

The Center for Irish Studies

10th March 2008

Mr. Alister McReynolds
Fellow, Institute of Ulster-Scots Studies
University of Ulster (Magee)
Northland Road
Londonderry BT48 7JL
Northern Ireland

Dear Alister:

This letter comes to express my heartfelt thanks for your seminal contributions as first keynoter at the 2008 Southern Conference of the American Conference for Irish Studies. The event occurred on 6th – 8th March 2008 at the Coastal Georgia Center, beside the historic district of the city of Savannah, Georgia—one of the most Irish settlements in the United States. Scholars from over 55 discrete North American, Irish, and British universities gave papers at the Conference, offering carefully researched and acutely compelling insights into the Irish and Scots-Irish experience, both on the island of Ireland and abroad.

As I mentioned in welcoming remarks, Irish Studies and the greater Irish consciousness are increasingly dedicated to accurate, cogent, and nuanced engagement with Scots-Irish history, culture, and accomplishment. As regards advancing that trend and ambition within the American Conference for Irish Studies, I cannot think of a better speaker than your good self. Your major address to the Conference was an exemplary piece of scholarship: meticulously crafted; entirely comprehensible; and supremely relevant. Scores of conference attendees commented positively about it, several being particularly pleased with its placement as the threshold occurrence—brilliant and inspirational.

I sincerely hope that your various contributions to the Conference throughout its run represent only the beginning of a long, strong relationship between our Center for Irish Studies and the Institute of Ulster-Scots Studies.

With great gratitude,

Howard Keeley PhD
Director, Center for Irish Studies

Exploring Diverse Irish Identities through a Student-Focused Culture of Engagement

University of Southern Georgia Center for Irish Studies. Letter of appreciation.

L-R. Julia Lane, John Mann, Alister McReynolds, Michael McReynolds. Harrington Graveyard - Stone commemorataes a shipwreck and the deaths of five local men led by Scots Irish Captain William Sproul.

Television presenter F. Ferrell and Professor John Wilson, Brunswick, Maine.

Professor John Wilson and John Mann, Brunswick, Maine.

Professor John Wilson, television interview. Brunswick, Maine.

Julia Lane, Alister McReynolds, John Mann. Harrington Meeting House (Presbyterian) Pemaquid, Maine.

Maine's Islands and Peninsulas.

Damariscotta, Maine.

Maine's lobster-fishing coastline.

Maine coastal settlement.

Fidelma McCarron, John Mann, Alister McReynolds and Dr. Ed McCarron outside Maine Historical Society, Longfellow House, Portland, Maine. Ed and Fidelma are historians who have written about Irish and Scots Irish settlements in Maine.

The Smithsonian Associates

Friday, June 16, 2006

Dear Alister,

It was a pleasure working with you on the Scots-Irish event. The program was greatly enjoyed by our participants. Your ability to express your thoughts clearly for the general public and your the command of your subject, were excellent! All and all, it added up to a wonderful program. Quality presenters like you is what makes the Smithsonian Associates a world leader in adult learning. We appreciate you sharing your time and talent with us.

Best Regards,

Pam

Pam

Letter of appreciation from Smithsonian Institute, Washington DC.

Scots Irish Museum, Brunswick, Maine.

Tower at Fort William Henry, Maine (near New Harbor).
Remamed Fort Frederick by Dunbar.

Harrington Meeting House.

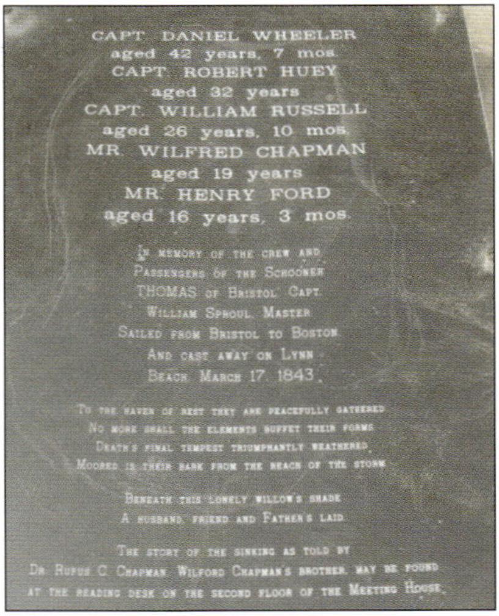

Gravestone at Harrington Meeting House which commemorates five local men who were shipwrecked.

11

Lewis And Clark Expedition - The Ulster Scots Contribution

As an amateur scientist long before he became President, Thomas Jefferson entertained an active curiosity about the vast unexplored American wilderness that lay to the North and West of the Mississippi River.

So it was that in 1803 President Jefferson persuaded Congress to commission an expedition that mapped and catalogued the scenery, horticulture, wildlife and native peoples of this area. The expedition lasted for three years and was led by twenty nine year old Meriwether Lewis and his fellow Virginian Captain William Clark whose Scots Irish antecedents hailed from Upperlands in Co. Londonderry.

Lewis was of Welsh extraction but was taught in school by James Waddell who was born in Newry in July 1739 and who as a child had subsequently emigrated to Pennsylvania.

The expedition was largely made up of military men of whom there where about fifty in number. At one point the Corps was obliged to live with Native American Sioux tribesmen and encountered all manner of danger including attacks by grizzly bears.

Not only was the expedition important for educational reasons but it gave the U.S. legal claim to the 'Oregon territory' under the valid criteria of 'Discovery and Explanation'.

Of the Expedition Corps at least five were of Ulster Scots background.

William Bratton who was born in 1778 in Augusta County Virginia was a hunter, blacksmith and gunsmith. During the course of the expedition he worked closely with fellow Ulster Scots descendant – John Shields of Kentucky who was a gunsmith, blacksmith and boat-builder. Of similar background Private Alexander Carson was the uncle of the famous Scots Irish cavalry scout and Indian fighter – Christopher 'Kit' Carson. Alexander Carson was born in Mississippi in 1775.

Private Hugh McNeal was another of the Scots Irish contingent who joined the Corps on April 1st 1804. He continued to serve in the Army after the expedition and enlisted in the Infantry in 1811.

Private George Shannon was born in Pennsylvania in 1785 and was the youngest member of the expedition at eighteen years old. After his return he became a lawyer and served for a period as a senator. During the expedition Shannon often got lost but always managed to find his way back to the expedition. Captain Clark once stated that Shannon was, "one of the most active and useful men we had".

Christopher Columbus may or may not have discovered America but what is for certain is that the Ulster Scots contributed hugely to the claiming, mapping and charting of all that lies 'Out West' – including the magnificent Rocky Mountains.

12

Robert Fulton - Pennsylvanian Engineer and Developer of Steamboat Transport

Of all the significant American engineers and inventors, who emerged from amongst the ranks of the Scots Irish, probably the greatest was Robert Fulton. Although Fulton was born in a Pennsylvania farm house in 1765, not all of his projects were carried out in the United States. Instead both France and England served as laboratories for Fulton's early inventive projects.

Robert Fulton's ancestral family originally hailed from Ayrshire and settled in the Lisburn area sometime between 1611 and 1614, this being the year when the Rev. Dr Fulton was appointed as Chaplain to Lady Arabella Stuart. She was the wife of the first Marquis of Hertford who held considerable lands around Lisburn. As a result of his services to the Hertford family Rev. Fulton was given a large farm at Belsize Lisburn. In the next generation Captain Richard Fulton of Blaris (which is on the western edge of Lisburn) raised a company of horse for King William's cause during the Glorious Revolution campaign in Ireland. Incidentally Richard Fulton's second son John became Registrar of the Supreme Court of Calcutta and his brother Thomas, who was born in 1663 at Blaris, was Presbyterian Minister in Lisburn in 1693.

So the family was well established around Lisburn when Robert Fulton's ancestor emigrated to the US sometime around the year 1700.

In what might be viewed as archetypal of Scots Irish ambition and drive the family soon became established in the town renowned as the home of Scots Irish American President James Buchanan - Lancaster Pennsylvania. By 1735 Robert Fulton's father had held various positions of trust and public office there including that of Secretary of the Union of Fire Officers. He was a strict Presbyterian and one of the founders of the Presbyterian Church in Lancaster.

Robert Fulton left home at age 18 and headed for Philadelphia. There he opened a studio where he successfully plied his talent for miniature portrait painting. Fortunately this may have been how he met Benjamin Franklin, with whose encouragement and introductions he moved to London in 1786. It was there that he developed his Art to such an extent that he exhibited at the Royal Gallery in 1791. But Fulton's ambitions were truly those of 'Renaissance Man'. And so shortly afterwards he switched his attention to canal construction. However this was a short-term interest and by 1793 he was designing steam-powered ships.

Unfortunately the British Navy personnel were not particularly impressed by his designs and so in 1797 he moved once more – this time to France. He began working there on the development of submarines. In 1800 he advanced this revolutionary idea when he piloted the 'Nautilus' for 17 minutes in water that was 25 foot deep. Always restless he returned to England in 1804 again and began to design submarines for the

British Navy, who were by now much impressed with his new ideas. His work for the navy extended into the development of the technology and power of torpedoes. This was dramatically demonstrated in tests when Fulton blew up an empty 300 ton ship.

After living in Europe for 19 years Robert Fulton eventually returned to the U.S. in 1806. He was granted $5,000 by Congress with which he was to carry out further experiments on behalf of the Nation. President Jefferson specifically requested his help with building canals in the newly acquired Louisiana territory. Fulton politely declined this request for the very good reason that he had decided to concentrate on, 'the steamboat project', once and for all.

Firstly he contracted with James Watt's firm in England for the supply of better steam engine models. This purchase alone cost $20,000. On August 17th 1807 Fulton made the maiden steam boat voyage from New York to Albany. The journey took 32 hours to complete with two hours being shaved off the return trip. Fulton's model steam boat was patented in 1809. It was to revolutionize travel on the great rivers of the USA – particularly of course - the Mississippi.

Fulton's final major undertaking was the development of the steam-powered warship – 'The Demalogus' which was patented in 1813.

Shortly afterwards in February 1815 Robert Fulton died as a result of complications which set in after a winter cold. As a mark of respect members of both Houses of Congress wore mourning and businesses in New York City closed for the day.

Thus ended a creative and full life led by the man that many Americans have come to view as their own Scots Irish Leonardo da Vinci.

Cyrus McCormick 1809-1884

13

Cyrus McCormick 1809-1884

Cyrus McCormick's great-grandfather Thomas McCormick emigrated from Dergina near Ballygawley Co. Tyrone to Pennsylvania in 1730's and Polly the inventor's mother could trace her lineage to Co Armagh in the late 1640's.

In 1779 Cyrus' grandfather Robert moved his wife Martha and their five children from Cumberland County Pennsylvania to Virginia where he bought a log house and 450 acres of land near the Rockbridge / Augusta County line in the Shenandoah Valley. This lies just to the west side of the Blue Ridge Mountains. It was here that his son Robert, the inventor's father was born just one year later in 1780. By 1812 the elder Robert owned a gristmill, a sawmill, a cider mill, a distillery, two grain mills and a smokehouse. As was the way with many Scots Irish at this time the family grew and prospered in this new environment.

For a time Robert junior and Polly lived in the home place before they moved out to build a brick manor house in the

Robert McCormick, father of Cyrus

summer of 1822 when young Cyrus was just 13 years of age. It is said that Polly, “filled the house with mahogany furniture” and Robert bought from his father the 532 acres home farm – ‘Walnut Grove’. This farm near Raphine Virginia became a test farm for the school that was then known as Virginia Polytechnic Institute and State University and which is better known today as ‘Virginia Tech’. The blacksmith’s workshop at this site became a crucible of invention.

When the family had lived at ‘Walnut Grove’ for just two years Cyrus, whilst still a lad of 15, invented a lightweight cradle for harvesting grain. Since 1815 Cyrus’ father had been working on a horse-drawn reaper prototype. By 1831 he realised that he personally had taken the project as far as he could. Polly encouraged her son to help his father to ‘iron out’ any snags or hitches. Cyrus took to this work with ‘gusto’ and over the next six weeks he worked late into the night to be ready for the harvest season. His methods were thorough and painstaking. If a strand of wheat became entangled in the

McCormick house at Walnut Grove

Cyrus McCormick Reaper model

wheels Cyrus got down on his hand and knees and worked to determine exactly what had caused this to happen. Jo Anderson – his faithful African –American assistant was ever at his side to enable him to overcome every obstacle that he encountered. So it was that the 'improved reaper' was demonstrated in 1831 and patented in 1834 in time to ward off competition from Obadiah Hussey who was independently developing a similar concept.

In 1847 the inventor, who was also by now a wealthy and skilled businessman, moved to Chicago. It was a logical move. The 'Windy City' served the vast prairie grain fields of the mid-West. Cyrus' brothers Leander and William joined him there and the move soon paid dividends.

The site of the McCormick factory, Chicago, following the fire

In 1843 McCormick had sold 29 reapers and by 1846 this figure had risen to 75. In 1849, just two years after the move to Chicago the company sold 1,500 reapers and by 1859 the sales figure was 4,100 reapers. McCormick introduced innovative business practices such as 'no haggle' pricing, credit and financing, and money back guarantees on performance. He also developed a range of interchangeable replacement parts. His products came on to the market just at the very time that the railroad emerged as a means of delivery right across the United States and Canada. McCormick also gave his salesmen focussed training so that they were able to demonstrate the machines in the fields.

Today it is interesting to note that less than 2% of American's population is engaged in farming compared with 1831 when it was necessary for 90% of the population to farm in order to meet America's needs. Thus people were 'freed' to engage in other pursuits such as manufacturing, business, science, arts and service industries. All of these have contributed to improving the quality of life experience.

Cyrus McCormick the young Scots Irish American who became a millionaire at the age of 26, made a highly significant contribution to the creation of that quiet revolution.

Historic landmark plaque.

Edmund McIlhenny

14

Edmund McIlhenny and His Tabasco Sauce

SIGNIFICANT claims have been made as to the contribution which the Ulster Scots have made to civilization. Certainly in food and drink categories the carrying to The New World of our own varieties of skillet breads and whiskey deserves to be recognised. But do the Scots Irish in America receive sufficient recognition for the development of the still popular hot red pepper sauce known as Tabasco? Even today examination of the label of this product will reveal the name of the McIlhenny family and the Tabasco Company of Avery Island Louisiana.

Edmund McIlhenny was born on October 15th 1815 far from Louisiana in Hagerstown Maryland where he was the second eldest of nine sons born to John and Ann McIlhenny. John McIlhenny was fourth generation Scots Irish, the family having moved from Scotland to Ulster, mainly to the Raphoe area of Donegal just before 1700. Some members of the family, including Edmund's antecedents, emigrated to America within the ensuing 30 years. Edmund McIlhenny was born in a tiny

John Avery McIlhenny

apartment on the North Eastern corner of the town square above what is today a café known as 'The Skyline Coffee Co.' It was then know as McIlhenny's Tavern and run by Edmund's father John who was later to become Mayor of the town and a doctor in General Practice in Hagerstown. Indeed it was in this latter role that he contracted Asiatic cholera from a patient and died in 1832. At this point in his life young Edmund left school in order to help his widowed mother and took a job as a messenger for a bank in Baltimore. In mid 1837 there was an economic panic which decimated Baltimore's banks. Undaunted by this downturn Edmund McIlhenny obtained a letter of introduction to the Bank of Louisiana in New Orleans and in 1841 he headed south in the direction of , 'The Big Easy'. This particular bank was the third largest in the State at the time and Edmund McIlhenny was a hardworking and intelligent employee. Consequently he rose from being a humble bookkeeper to the position of General Agent, which involved monitoring five branches in Louisiana; at Baton Rouge, Francisville, Donaldsonville, Opelousas and Alexandria. Eventually he owned several banks. A confidential document from 1860 shows that he was then worth $112,000 which equates to around $2.5 million in today's money.

In June 1859 Edmund McIlhenny married Mary Elizabeth Avery on Petit Anse Island Louisiana. He was 44 years old and had become a wealthy New Orleans banker. His bride was 20 years his junior and even more wealthy. Her father Judge Daniel Dudley Avery had transformed Petit Anse from barren ground into a model farm and Plantation with sugar-cane being the key crop. This New Iberia area of Louisiana boasted a rich soil and doubly so in that it sat on a huge and accessible deposit of salt. In a sense this was a mixed blessing as it made the facility a prime acquisition during The American Civil War. Salt was used extensively for curing hides and preserving meats. These processes were vital to the military effort on both sides of the conflict. The McIlhenny family realised that this was the case and vacated their Avery Island estates and sought refuge in Texas to 'sit out 'the War down there. Eventually in 1863 Union soldiers stormed Avery Island and its salt mine on top of which The Confederates had built an extensive barracks. By 1865 the sugar cane crops had been destroyed and the Mansion House looted and 'trashed'. After the War, Edmund McIlhenny and his family moved back to the Avery Island residence, which had become very dilapidated. There Edmund attempted to revive both the house and his banking career. The results in both cases could best be described as dilatory. In this difficult time Edmund spent his days, deep in thought, tending to the Avery Island kitchen garden. However his fortune was altered dramatically in a New Orleans tavern one evening when a former Confederate soldier named Gleason, who had sought refuge from the Civil War in Mexico, casually gave him a handful of hot red peppers with which to flavour his food. However Edmund McIlhenny had more ambitious plans for these humble plants than simply to fry them for his supper that evening. Using the salt on which

Avery Island stood he began to experiment with the peppers and others which he had grown from the seeds within the pods. Single-handedly he turned the abandoned Confederacy Barracks inside the estate into what was virtually a food-science laboratory. Initially he prepared the first batch using new but empty Cologne bottles fitted with a shaker/sprinkler fixture as it was obvious that this fiery concoction was not a 'pouring' sauce in the conventional sense. The sauce was named 'Tabasco', which was a Mexican Indian word and the name of a place in Mexico that people in New Orleans knew to be renowned as a source of peppers and spices. Other hot pepper sauces existed in Louisiana and in other states at the time but these used radically different methods of production, which usually involved boiling, whereas Tabasco was the product of fermentation in white wine vinegar. So it was that in 1868 the brand started with 658 bottles. By 1889 the Company's annual production was in the order of 41,472 Tabasco sauce bottles. The Company's

Tabasco crockery stoneware jars

Tabasco Saucebottle and lable

historian Dr Shane Bernard has commented that when Edmund McIlhenny died aged 75 on November 25th 1890 none of his obituaries mentioned the development of Tabasco as being of any significance nor did he himself in the autobiographical sketch that he wrote a few years before his demise. Today's President and CEO of the Tabasco McIlhenny Company is Paul McIlhenny and the family still run the Company and refuse to sell out to the big food conglomerates.

The sobriquet which on a couple of levels comes to mind in relation to the achievement of Edmund McIlhenny and his Scots Irish family is that of , 'salt of the earth'.

Dan McCook

The Fighting McCooks

15

The Fighting McCooks

Up in the North Antrim, around the Ballymoney and Armoy area, the McCook family has long had a well-deserved reputation as champion long-distance runners. Their cousins in America are also renowned albeit for reasons other than their athletic ability. Writing in *The Proceedings of the Scotch–Irish Society in America,* Henry Howe applauded the family as follows – "One of the best-known Scotch–Irish families who have contributed their full share to the honorable record of that race in the United States are the Ohio McCooks, who acquired a wide reputation during the Civil War as the 'Fighting McCooks'."

The first of this family George McCook was born in 1752 near Ballymoney Co. Antrim. His grandfather, also George, had moved to and settled in this area having been born in Scotland. George the younger was subsequently to emigrate to America in the mid to late 1780's. By 1790 he had settled in York County Pennsylvania prior to moving to Canonsburg in Washington

McCook house, Ohio

County in the same state. He married Mary McCormick, originally from Glasgow, and they were the parents of four children – George (b.1795), Daniel (b.1798), John James (b.1806) and Mary who was born after 1806.

In 1825 Daniel and John James moved to Ohio with Dan settling in New Lisbon and John James in Steubenville. Daniel later moved to Carrolton where the house which he built in 1837 is today an historic site which is open to the public and is managed by the Carroll County Historical Society.

Daniel McCook and his eight sons, "the tribe of Dan" and John and his five sons, "the tribe of John" – fifteen men of Ohio all served in the Union Army during the Civil War. Daniel's family included five generals and brother John's brood two generals and three officers. Four of Daniel's family, including himself, died in the conflict. The courage and constancy of the McCooks brought honour and fame to the family. Those that survived the war added to this becoming congressmen, ambassadors, doctors, lawyers, ministers and scholars in civilian life.

Daniel McCook, the patriarch of the 'tribe of Dan' was commissioned as a major and lost his life in the battle of Buffington Island in 1863 when he led an advance party against

Confederate General John Morgan. Dan's son George Wythe McCook attained the rank of brigadier-general. After the war he was Attorney General for the state of Ohio and Democratic candidate for the same state for Congress in 1871. Other members of the tribe of Dan included Latimer, Robert, Alexander, Daniel Jr., Edwin Stanton, Charles Morris and John James. Latimer was a surgeon Major who was seriously wounded twice and who survived the war but died later in 1869 of debility associated with his wounds. Robert who was a lawyer and became Colonel of 9th Ohio Regiment was severely wounded in the battle of Mills Spring Kentucky and was shortly afterwards promoted to General. He was shot by Confederate guerillas as he lay wounded and prostrate in his ambulance wagon sick-bed. Alexander became a major general and survived the war. Edwin also earned the rank of major general. Although he was severely wounded three times he also survived the war. He eventually became Governor of the North Dakota Territory and was shot dead by a member of the audience when he was chairing an open public meeting. Daniel McCook became a brigadier-general and was killed in 1864 at the battle of Kennesaw Mountain. Charles Morris was the first McCook to be slain in the war at the first battle of Bull Run in July 1861. He was just 18 years of age when he was killed. John James survived the war, attaining the rank of Colonel.

The 'tribe of John' included the patriarch John who served as a surgeon during the war. Other members of this family who served were Edward, Anson, Henry, John James and Roderick. All of this family survived the war. Edward and Anson both attained the rank of major general. After the war Anson moved to New York City where as well as working as a lawyer he represented the Eighth New York District in Congress as a member of the Republican Party. He became Secretary of the United States Senate. Edward was appointed US Minister to the

Anson McCook

Sandwich Islands. He was twice Governor of Colorado, Henry and John James each attained the rank of Lieutenant and served as chaplains in the Union army. One was as Episcopalian rector and the other a Presbyterian minister. John James later became a Professor of Modern Languages in Trinity College Hartford. Roderick became a commander in the United States Navy.

Such was the impact of the McCook family's history on the American psyche that as late as June 1903 the editor of the New York Tribune could write, "The appellation of 'the fighting McCooks' is still almost as familiar as his own name to every American boy".

16

Kit Carson

CHRISTOPHER (Kit) Houston Carson was born on Christmas Eve 1809 in Richmond, Madison County Kentucky. His ancestor (great great grandfather) Rev. Alexander Harvey Carson was a Presbyterian Minister who was born in Scotland in 1683 and had been 'called' to Ulster where he met his future wife Sarah. Their eldest son John was born in 1710 but it was his younger brother Samuel who was Kit's great grandfather. Samuel was born in Co. Down in what family memory in America recalled, not very accurately, as "a small town now deserted at the foot of some mountains not far from Newry". The family moved from there with the Scots Irish Diaspora and landed in Pennsylvania which is where Samuel died in York County in 1759. His son William later moved to Iredell County North Carolina, which is where his son Lindsay, who was Kit's father was born. He it was who made the Carson home in Kentucky. And soon they moved again, as was the way with these restless people, to Franklin Missouri. Here Kit grew up and was apprenticed to a saddle maker.

Kit Carson

At 15 years of age 'Kit', the most restless of the whole clan, headed west for New Mexico. Thereafter he worked as a guide, a trapper a military scout, Indian agent, soldier (Brevet Brigadier General) and rancher. Hit initial renown came through a meeting with John C. Fremont who was on an expedition to map the western trails of the Pacific Ocean. The meeting took place quite by chance when Kit was on a family trip with his daughter. In his memoirs Fremont recalled the meeting quite vividly – "I was pleased with him and his manner of address at this first meeting. He was a man of medium height, broad shouldered and deep chested, with a clear steady blue eye and frank speech and address; quiet and unassuming."

After his trapping days were over Kit Carson settled in Taos New Mexico. After his second wife, an Arapahoe Native American died Kit's life was changed. He received instruction from Padre Antonio José Martinez and in 1842 was baptized into the Catholic Church. He became engaged to, and in 1843, married his third wife - the fourteen year old Josefa Jaramillo who came from a prominent Taos family. Kit and Josefa raised fifteen children the descendants of whom still live today in the Arkansas Valley of Colorado.

As regards military service Carson fought against the Mexicans in California in the 1840's alongside John C. Fremont and served under General Stephen Watts Kearny at the Battle of San Pascual where the Americans were defeated.

During the American Civil War, which first erupted in 1861, Carson resigned as a federal Indian agent for New Mexico and offered to help organize New Mexico's Volunteer Infantry in support of the Union. Slavery was not a practical reality in New Mexico due to the nature and needs of the environment. Carson

Kit Carson with John C Fremont

Kit Carson

was given the rank of Colonel of Volunteers and fought under the command of General R S Canby.

The most controversial period of Carson's life was that relating to his dealings with Native Americans. During the Navajo campaign, and acting on the orders of General James H Carleton, Carson operated a 'scorched earth' policy against the Navajo. In this he used other Native American tribes, such as the Utes, to attack the Navajo. The Navajo were virtually 'starved out' of existence. Their livestock, crops and food supplies were destroyed. In 1864 he forced 8000 Navajo men, women and children to march 300 miles to Fort Sumner New Mexico. The 'Long Walk' became for the Navajo what the 'trail of tears' had been for the Cherokee. In 1868 the Navajo were allowed to return to their New Mexico reservation which still exists today.

In that same year of 1864 Carson was sent by General Carleton to 'deal' with the Native Americans in West Texas. He met a combined force of 1500 Kiowa, Comanche and Cheyenne warriors at the ruins of Adobe Walls. Carson inflicted heavy losses on the attacking warriors using mountain howitzers for the purpose. He then burned their camps and lodges.

When the Civil War and Indian campaigns had ceased Kit Carson took up ranching – eventually settling in Boggsville near Franksville Colorado. He died at Fort Lyon Colorado May 23rd 1868.

Carson's early reputation was positive and he was to become the hero of dime novels, poems and films. In 1856 Albert Richardson described him as being, "a gentleman of instinct, upright, pure and simple hearted, beloved alike by Indians, Mexicans and Americans."

In the last twenty five years however Carson's reputation has been revised and is viewed by some observers as being more malign. Others have argued that he moderated the more extreme genocidal tendencies and plans of General Carleton. The 1990 song by singer/songwriter Bruce Cockburn hauntingly expresses the sometimes contradictory image of the man -

> "Kit Carson was a hero to some
> With his poison and his flame
> But somewhere there's a restless ghost
> That used to bear his name".

17

Samuel Wesley Fordyce

Samuel Wesley Fordyce's grandfather, for whom he was named, was born in Armoy Co. Antrim on October 17th 1734. He emigrated to Washington County Pennsylvania in 1775 and died in Greene County in the same state in 1824.

With certainty the Fordyce family could trace their Armoy background to 8th November 1643 when John Fordyce was born in the North Antrim village. There is some evidence to suggest that the family had travelled from Scotland to settle there as much as 100 years earlier. It is definite however that on 7th April 1668, 25 year old John Fordyce married Margaret Bane, who was also reared in the village in which they were wed. Their son Hugh was born in Armoy on December 14th 1675 and it is from this line that Samuel Wesley Fordyce was descended. His grandfather's emigration to Pennsylvania in 1775 was not the first such venture as in an earlier generation Peter Fordyce left Armoy and settled in Parrsburgh Nova Scotia. Samuel Wesley Fordyce was born in Guernsey County Ohio on

Samuel Wesley Fordyce, Armoy ancestor

February 7th 1840. His parents John and Mary Ann had moved from their neighbouring home state of Pennsylvania and settled there. Samuel Wesley Fordyce's life was to be one in which he built many thousands of miles of railroad as well as numerous banks and businesses and in which he was to be a counsellor and advisor to every President from Lincoln up and until the time of his death on August 3rd 1919 when he was in his 79th year.

Sam Fordyce was born into a family of ten children and was educated initially at local schools before attending Madison College in Uniontown Pennsylvania and then heading to North Illinois University in Henry Illinois. When he returned home to Ohio he took up a position as Station Agent for the Central Ohio

Railroad. It was indeed a lowly position for a man who was to be the principal developer of railroads across America after The Civil War.

When the War broke out Sam Fordyce joined the Union Army initially enlisting as a member of the First Ohio Volunteer Cavalry. He joined as a Private but was later promoted to First Lieutenant of Company B ~ First Ohio Volunteer Cavalry.

His next promotion came in 1863 when he was awarded command of Company H and a few months later was advanced to the position of Inspector General of Cavalry in the Army of the Cumberland and assigned to the Second Cavalry Division under command of General George Crook.

Sam Fordyce fought at the Battles of Murfreesboro and Chickamauga under General Rosecrans and General Buell and also in Kentucky at Shiloh and Perryville. At these Battles and in other minor skirmishes he was always in the thickest of the fight. He was three times wounded and three times captured by the enemy although he was speedily recaptured twice and escaped on the other occasion. After the Civil War Sam Fordyce moved south, in more ways than one, and settled first in St Louis Missouri where he aided the building and financing of The St Louis Valley line, which is now part of the Missouri Pacific system. He also cooperated in the building of the St Louis and San Francisco system and the Missouri and Oklahoma and Gulf Railroad. This period of his life found him based in Missouri but involved in railway building from Mexico to Denver Colorado and on to Illinois and Minnesota. Although seen as a 'man of the North', Sam Fordyce refused to be confined by the battle lines of the Civil War and saw the entire United States as his context and the building of railroads across its length and breadth as key to the economic recovery of the country following the debilitation and destruction caused by the War.

Samuel and Susan Fordyce

Shortly after this Fordyce settled in Huntsville Alabama and there he married Susan E. Chadick whose father had been a Presbyterian Minister in the Confederate forces during the War. Still suffering gravely from the wounds that he had attained during the Civil War Sam Fordyce moved again to Arkansas in January 1873 and established his home in the mountains near Hot Springs. He was convinced that the healing properties of the waters there would be beneficial to his physical weakness resultant from his wounds. So perilous was his situation that during the previous year he had been given only six months to live. After being 'cured' by the waters Fordyce moved his family to there and began seriously investing in the city including building the famous 'Fordyce Bathhouse'. He said, 'I felt I owed my life to Hot Springs'. The Fordyce Bathhouse opened in 1915 and as well as Springs it boasted a library, a music room, and two bowling alleys .Since 1988 the bathhouse of yesteryear has operated as a museum and visitor centre.

Incidentally it was to this city in 1953 that a 7 year old boy named Billy Blythe moved from the town of Hope, some 80 miles away in the same state. He was later to become known to all of us as President Bill Clinton.

Once settled in Hot Springs Samuel Fordyce used his influence to settle disputed land claims and prevailed on General John A. Logan who was a U.S. Senator to introduce a Bill which resulted in the erection of the, 'state of the art', Army and Navy Hospital in the town. When it came to establishing the railroad system for the state of Arkansas Sam Fordyce rode over the route to gain, 'right of way' where this was needed and to gain 'first hand' knowledge about the countryside. In this process he was as economical as possible and in particular used roads that had already been cut by Civil War soldiers as well as the narrow log roads which led from the lumber camps into the cities and towns. Very often these were 'wash board' roads that were built over swampy ground. Thus he built terminals in Arkansas towns such as Marmaduke and Paragould.

As well as those states already mentioned the 'Lone Star State' of Texas also benefited hugely from the business expertise of Sam Fordyce. This was particularly true as regards the cities of Dallas and Denison where Fordyce invested in and built the first 'Cotton Compress 'in both those two cities. The Cotton Compress industry developed in antebellum Texas because of the need to lower the cost of transporting cotton on sailing vessels. Prior to the use of compressors or hydraulics the bulky cotton bales had been physically parcelled and trussed into shape by men known as 'screw jacks'. The use of the Cotton Compress reduced the size of these bulky misshapen bales by half and as Sam Fordyce recognised this eased the transport of cotton bales by railroad freight. In Texas this made a huge impact on the cotton industry. Not much is written about cotton in Texas and yet as recently as 1979 cotton contributed $ 1 billion to the Texas economy and represented 10% of the agricultural produce of the state.

Building on this innovation Sam Fordyce set up the Texas and St. Louis Railroad Company of Arkansas, which was incorporated on May 21st 1881 and the line ran from Texarkana Texas to the Arkansas Missouri line.

Sam Fordyce went on to hold various key positions in the railroad business including that of Vice President and Treasurer of the Texas and St Louis Railway, President of the Western Railway, President of the Kansas City Pittsburgh and Gulf Railway, and the Little Rock, Hot Springs and Western Railroad.

It is estimated that overall Sam Fordyce financed or assisted with the building of at least 24,000 miles of railway across and zigzagging the American continent.

Chief Street, Fordyce, Arkanas

As a result of his achievements with the railroads Sam Fordyce had a number of streets and towns named after him. The small town of Sam Fordyce near La Joya Texas in Hidalgo County contains the Sam Fordyce Elementary School which is still active today and is located at the western end of the St. Louis Brownsville and Mexico Railway. Predictably there is the town of Fordyce in Arkansas which was built in 1882 when the aforementioned Cotton Belt route was constructed. It is situated on US167 heading south and is the 'county seat' for Dallas County Arkansas.

Sam Fordyce had business interests other than railroads including the Light and Power Company of St Louis, the Jefferson Hotel Company, the Hot Springs Street Railway Company and was a Director of the American Rio Grande Land and Irrigation Company of Texas. This was the largest irrigation and canal system ever built in the United States. He was also President of the Houston Oil Company.

Although Sam Fordyce fought for the North during the Civil War he was nonetheless a member of the Democratic Party and was often solicited to run for political office which he always declined. Similarly when his friend President McKinley

Sam Fordyce in later years.

(g-g grandson of an emigrant from Dervock near Armoy) offered to make Sam Fordyce Ambassador to Russia he declined the honour.

Sam Fordyce's manner was affable and he was widely respected. His story is key to understanding the contribution that the Scots Irish made to building the United States.

He was progressive and positive and most of all forward-looking in his determination not to be held back by the divisions that had racked his country during the Civil War.

It was not an attitude that was unique to him, or that he had invented, for after all it could be argued that his grandfather Samuel Fordyce who left Armoy in 1775 had been motivated by these very same forces.

18

WHO'S THE GOVERNOR?

MOST people know that a disproportionately large number of Unites States Presidents have been of Ulster descent. Less well known however, are the State Governors who were of Scots Irish origin.

The list below (although not wholly exhaustive) gives an insight into the extent of this phenomenon. It does not include those Presidents of Scots-Irish origin who were also State Governors e.g. Theodore Roosevelt, Ronald Reagan and George W. Bush.

Alabama	**Robert Miller Patton** (1809-85) 17th Governor – Ulster Scot on his father's side and Scottish on his mother's.
Colorado	**Edward Moody McCook**, 5th and 7th Governor (1869-73, 1874-75). He also served in the Civil War and attained the rank of Brigadier – General. Also acting Governor of 'Dakota Territory'.

Delaware - **Charles Polk** (1788-1857), 13th Governor (1827-30), and President of the Constitutional Convention of his State in 1831.

John P Cochran (1809-98), 26th Governor (1857-79)

Idaho **John Henry Brady** (b.1862), 8th Governor (1910-11)

David P Thompson, 9th Governor of the State (1874-76) – built the first railroad in the nearby State of Oregon and was twice Mayor of the City of Portland in that State.

Illinois **William Lee Davidson Ewing** (1795-1846) Senator and acting Governor (1834).

Iowa **James Wilson Grimes** (1812-72) 3rd Governor (1854-58).

Albert Baird Cummins (1850-1926)18th Governor (1901-08)

Kansas **John Alexander Martin** (1839-89) 9th Governor (1885-89).

Maine **Robert Pinckney Dunlap** (1794-1859), 8th Governor.

Hugh Johnston Anderson (1801-81), 14th Governor (1844-47).

Abner Coburn (1803-85), 24th Governor.

Minnesota **Alexander Ramsey**, 1st territorial and second State Governor (1849-53, 1860-64) was the grandson of a Scots Irishman who served in the Revolutionary War.

Missouri **Trusten Polk** (1811-73) of the same Scots Irish origins as President Polk and was 11th Governor (1857).

Nebraska **James E Boyd** (b1834), 8th Governor (1891-92), was himself born in Co Tyrone.

New Hampshire **Jeremiah Smith**, 4th Governor (1809-10). His son and namesake was an Associate Justice of the Supreme Court.

Samuel Bell (1770-1850) a descendant of one of Ulster Scots settlers of 1718 was three times elected Governor (1819-23) with little or no opposition.

John Bell brother of Samuel was 13th Governor (1828-29)

Joseph Merill Harper (1789-1865) was acting Governor in 1831.

Samuel Dinsmoor (1766-1835), 16th Governor (1831-33) was a distinguished factor of the State and was of Scots Irish descent on both sides of his family.

His eldest son and namesake **Samuel Dinsmoor** (1799-1869) was 24th Governor (1849-52).

Noah Martin (1801-63) of Scots Irish descent on both sides of his parentage was 25th Governor.

Charles Bell son of Governor John and nephew of Governor Samuel was 41st Governor of State.

Governor W. Ewing

Governor S. Houston

Governor John P. Cochran

Governor N. Martin

Governor Robert Miller Patten

Governor E Boyd

Governor Edward McCook

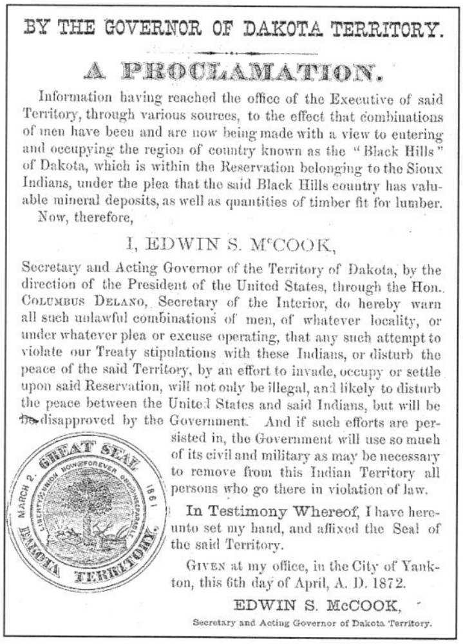

BY THE GOVERNOR OF DAKOTA TERRITORY.

A PROCLAMATION.

Information having reached the office of the Executive of said Territory, through various sources, to the effect that combinations of men have been and are now being made with a view to entering and occupying the region of country known as the "Black Hills" of Dakota, which is within the Reservation belonging to the Sioux Indians, under the plea that the said Black Hills country has valuable mineral deposits, as well as quantities of timber fit for lumber.

Now, therefore,

I, EDWIN S. M[c]COOK,

Secretary and Acting Governor of the Territory of Dakota, by the direction of the President of the United States, through the Hon. COLUMBUS DELANO, Secretary of the Interior, do hereby warn all such unlawful combinations of men, of whatever locality, or under whatever plea or excuse operating, that any such attempt to violate our Treaty stipulations with these Indians, or disturb the peace of the said Territory, by an effort to invade, occupy or settle upon said Reservation, will not only be illegal, and likely to disturb the peace between the United States and said Indians, but will be be disapproved by the Government. And if such efforts are persisted in, the Government will use so much of its civil and military as may be necessary to remove from this Indian Territory all persons who go there in violation of law.

In Testimony Whereof, I have hereunto set my hand, and affixed the Seal of the said Territory.

GIVEN at my office, in the City of Yankton, this 6th day of April, A. D. 1872.

EDWIN S. McCOOK,

Secretary and Acting Governor of Dakota Territory.

Proclamation from Edwin S McCook (as 'Acting' Governor of Dakota Territory

	John Butler Smith, 47th Governor (1893-95) was another descendant of one of the original Scots Irish settlers of New Hampshire of 1718.
Ohio	**Jeremiah Morrow** (1770-1852) was Governor from 1822-26. **Allen Trimble** (1783-1870) was Governor from 1826-30.
Oregon	**James Shields,** Territorial Governor (1848) born in Dungannon Co Tyrone.
Pennsylvania	**William Findlay** (1768-1846) 4th Governor (1817-20) was also United States Senator and Treasurer of the Mint at Philadelphia. **John White Geary** (1813-73) was Governor from 1867 to 1873.
South Carolina	**Patrick Noble** (1787-1840) was 30th Governor (1838-40) was grandson of an Ulster immigrant.
South Dakota	**Corie Isaac Crawford**, 6th Governor (1907-08).
Tennessee	**Samuel Houston**, 7th Governor (1827-28) – see under Texas for further details. **Benton McMillin** (b.1845) Governor (1899-1903) Envoy – Extraordinary and Minister - Plenipotentiary to Peru in 1913.

Texas

Samuel Houston (1793-1863) was a descendant of John Houston who settled in Philadelphia in 1689. He was a Member of Congress from Tennessee (1823-27), Governor of Tennessee (1827-28), and Commander-in –Chief of the Texans who defeated the Mexicans under Santa Anna in 1836 on the banks of the San Jacinto and thus achieved independence for Texas. He was elected President of the new republic in the same year, was re-elected in 1841, and in 1859 was elected Governor of the State. Houston the capital of Harris County, Texas was named in his honour.

Peter Hansborough Bell (1812-98) 3rd Governor (1849-53).

James Edward Ferguson (1874-1944) Governor (1915-17).

Vermont

Charles James Bell, 50th Governor 1905 was descended from one of the Londonderry, New Hampshire Settlers of 1718.

John Wolcott Stewart, 33rd Governor (1870-72) was descended from Robert Stewart who went from Edinburgh to Londonderry in Ulster and whose son also emigrated to Londonderry New Hampshire in 1718. His grandfather fought in the Revolutionary War.

West Virginia

William Erskine Stevenson (1820-1883) was 2nd Governor (1869-71).

Wisconsin

Henry Dodge, 1st and 4th Governor (1836-41) and (1845-48) was Scots Irish on his mother's side. Her name was Anne Nancy Hunter.

19

Jeremiah Morrow - Governor of Ohio

Jeremiah Morrow represented his adopted state of Ohio as its first Congressman, later as Senator and eventually in the period 1842-1846 as its 9th Governor.

Henry Clay said of him, "no man, in the sphere within which he acted ever commanded or deserved the implicit confidence of congress more that Jeremiah Morrow".

Ohio's tallest bridge is named after him and within his lifetime in 1848 both the County and the city of 'Morrow' were dubbed in his honour.

The Governor's grandfather, who was born in1712, was called Jeremiah **Murray** and was a Covenanter who had emigrated from Londonderry in 1730. He settled in the state of Pennsylvania near Gettysburg, in what was then known as York County, but is today called Adams County. He brought his deeply held faith with him and in 1753 Rev. John Cuthbertson conferred on him the position or Ruling Elder of the Rock Creek Covenanter Society. He was the father of several daughters and one son.

That son John, who was to become the father of the Governor, was a successful farmer and in 1750 it was he who changed the family name from the Scottish Murray (which originally derived from Moray as a 'geographical' Scottish surname) to Morrow. John Morrow was appointed as Commissioner of York County from 1791-1793 and died in 1811 as the father of nine children.

The eldest of those offspring was Jeremiah who was born on October 6th 1771. He spent his youth on his father's farm and attended the local public schools where he obtained a basic but good standard of education. He supplemented this by developing a lifelong habit of industrious reading and study. One summer he attended a College programme and it was there that be obtained his knowledge of Higher Mathematics and Surveying.

In the spring of 1795 Jeremiah moved to that part of the county which was then known as the 'Northwest territory' and is today the state of Ohio. He settled initially in Columbia at the mouth of the Little Miami River. Shortly afterwards he married his cousin Mary Parkhill of Fayette Co. Pennsylvania and subsequently brought her as his bride to Ohio.

Initially Jeremiah worked as a surveyor near the town of Foster on lands which had been acquired by other settlers. At that time the conurbation which is today the nearby city of Cincinnati was then little more that a village. Jeremiah also worked as a school teacher and as a farmer. In all these activities he worked with a high level of practical knowledge. However it was another profession, that of politics, which called to him and that is where he built his reputation.

When Jeremiah Morrow was elected as the first Congressman for the State of Ohio in the 1801-1802 session this was the first of many offices that he held over the next 40 years. He was initially a member of the Democratic - Republican Party

Jeremiah Morrow

and had campaigned hard for statehood for Ohio. During his two terms as Governor the National Road was extended into Ohio and work also commenced on the Ohio and the Erie and Miami canal systems. Morrow was one of the founders of the Whig Party in America. Even though Thomas Jefferson placed great reliance on him and he was a friend of Madison, Monroe, and John Quincy Adams, Jeremiah Morrow never disdained ordinary hard work. When the Duke of Saxe-Weimar visited him on his farm he was busily cutting a wagon pole and in 1825 when he welcomed La Fayette to Ohio as the Nation's guest he did so dressed in his everyday clothes.

From his early days Jeremiah Morrow was a member of the Associate Reformed Church and when he died aged 80 he was buried in Union Cemetery on Montgomery Pike with a plain headstone that was neither larger nor costlier than any other in the graveyard.

Describing his performance in Congress Henry Clay depicted Morrow's modest demeanour, "A few artless but sensible words, pronounced in his plain Scotch-Irish dialect, were always sufficient to insure the passage of any bill or resolution which he reported."

It is interesting to note how 120 years after his grandfather had emigrated from Londonderry, Jeremiah Morrow's dialect could be characterised in this way by a contemporary as being "Scotch-Irish" and how his personal characteristics so described embodied so much of the Scots Irish persona.

20

Scots Irish Cultural Influences

In a number of significant ways the cultural values developed by the Scots Irish during their time in Ulster shaped their cultural influence in the United States. This experience created a set of influences that were somewhat distinct from that brought to the shores of the New World by those Scots who travelled directly from their homeland to America. When these hardy travelling people moved the short distance from Scotland to Ulster they exchanged a society that was still largely feudal for a more individualistic way of life. This developed the self-confidence and 'can do' individualism of the Scots Irish which greatly enhanced their mastery of the American frontier.

In Ulster the Scots Irish also became more commercially aware than their 'cousins' back in Scotland as a result of their extensive involvement in the Ulster linen industry. This was an undertaking that required skills in production, processing and marketing. These were areas of generic skills which would prove to be crucial in building the business of America. Out of all of this grew a social and political philosophy that was all about individual rights and the forms of Government that emerged from the Scottish enlightenment.

The Scots Irish shared with the Scots a belief in the importance of Education and a wariness of all 'rulers' particularly those associated with ecclesiastical forms of Government. Counter balancing these 'civilized' views were the cultural attitudes that arose out of the well-documented ruthlessness of the Scots Irish particularly when they were provoked. This capacity was demonstrated early in America's history during The Seven Years War and in Pontiac's War. This was a cultural influence that might well be disapproved of today but which was arguably intrinsic to the advancement of Western society in America.

In terms of the non-material cultural influence of the Scots Irish it was they who gave Appalachia the roots of its language, its 'Jack tales' and its country music. Throughout America the Scots Irish brought an enduring influence in the importance afforded to the family, to individualism and to public service.

In cultural terms probably the core legacy however has been the influence of evangelical Presbyterianism. This church/religious movement had developed in a unique way in Ulster that was quite distinct from that of Scotland due largely to the particular pressures faced by the Scots settlers in Ulster. Many commentators believe that these religious ideas as they were formulated in Ulster underlie the culture of much of the United States, most particularly in the 'Bible belt'. Specifically these particular influences cluster around the concepts of predestination and the strengthening ability of men to directly build their own covenant with God.

Overall the cultural influence of the Scots Irish in America, even when it seems to be almost imperceptible, is in fact inestimable in terms of its total impact.

21

John Armoy Knox

Nowadays when we in Ulster think of the North Antrim village of Armoy we naturally think of its most famous son as being the late Joey Dunlop – motorcycling champion and 'King of the Road'.

Long before Joey's time however Armoy had another famous son – an Ulster Scot who emigrated to the United States and who kept the name of the village to the forefront, incorporated as it was within his name – John Armoy Knox.

John Knox was born in Armoy on August 10th 1851, the son of Thomas and Jane McBride Knox. His father and uncle owned Armoy Flax and Grain mills plus land on the outskirts of the village at Park, Moyaver and Turnarobert.

Knox emigrated to the United States in 1871 for reasons of improving his health and settled in Austin Texas working initially as a sewing machine agent before starting to work for a newspaper. In 1875 he married Letitia McDonald and they had at least three children.

John Armoy Knox

In May 1881, along with Alexander E. Sweet, he founded, ‘Texas Siftings’ a humorous paper that had as its masthead – “Knox and Sweet, proprietors, editors and sifters”.

In early 1884, perhaps somewhat incongruously, ‘Texas Siftings’ moved to New York as its base where Knox managed the business side of the operation whilst Sweet provided more of the ‘literary’ input. This was a successful partnership and division of labour and from 1886-91 it became one of the most popular publications right across the United States with a circulation in the order of 150,000 copies. During this period it spread its wings sufficiently to have a branch office and a specific edition for London. However, circulation started to decline some time after this and the paper was eventually sold off in 1895.

During this period Knox was once more ‘on the move’ including a spell when he edited and managed the Atlanta Herald from 1892-1894. In 1896 he returned to New York where he continued to contribute articles to several newspapers and magazines.

Sitting alongside the journalism Sweet and Knox also published a number of books – many copies of which still exist and which fetch high prices being much sought after in the booming sales of what is termed ‘Americano’ in the antiques trade. The titles of the works portray why this is the case – ‘Sketches from Texas Siftings’ was published in 1885 whilst the wonderfully entitled ‘On a Mexican mustang through Texas from the Gulf to the Rio Grande’, was published in 1883. A number of books in similar vein were published during these years.

In 1883 Knox criticised D.B.Sheehan a New York sculptor for his reflections on local Government in Texas whereupon the two gentlemen fought a duel in which thankfully neither of them was injured. In 1900 Knox sought to enjoin actress Blanche Walsh from starring in a play called ‘MARCEL’ on the grounds that he had copyrighted a play of his own by that name. He lost the suit.

An interesting insight into Knox’s character is given in one of his quotes where he wrote, “Be virtuous and – you will get left”.

Ultimately Knox’s key contribution was to the creation of the myth of the cowboy and the old west. One commentator put it succinctly – “the cowboy, as a subject dominated Texas literature thereafter and entered the scene in the 1880’s. Alex E. Sweet and J. Armoy Knox treated cowboy lore in a humorous satirical fashion." Another writer noted that the observations of Sweet and Knox offered, "a grotesque view of the manners and customs in Texas. Some sober truths in the guise of fun."

As a young lad growing up in Armoy and playing Cowboys and Indians neither I nor my young pals had any idea that a local man, a man from our own village, had contributed so much to the making of the myths and stories of the old west that we were seeing in black and white on our television screens and re-enacting in the playground of Armoy Primary School which was not a hundred yards away from the ruins of the Armoy Flax and Grain mills.

22

Virginia Scots Irish Novelist - Ellen Glasgow - 'Vein of Iron'

In the United States, apart from Mark Twain, 'Southern' writers with Scots-Irish ancestry have included: William Faulkner, Thomas Wolfe, John Pendleton Kennedy, Carson McCullers, and the subject of this chapter – Ellen Glasgow. All of these individuals had other ethnic 'lines' of course and the tension which these cultural differences provoked within families was often the key to understanding the experience on which they drew to inform the lives of their fictional characters. Certainly that was the case with Ellen Glasgow whose distinguished novels are noted for their style and content. The Pulitzer-Prize winning novelist was born in Richmond Virginia in April 1873, the daughter of Francis Thomas Glasgow and Anne Jane Gholson Glasgow. Francis was descended from hardy Scots Irish stock who were early settlers in The Shenandoah Valley. He was raised in Rockbridge County and graduated from Washington and Lee College. Ellen Glasgow's mother was a member of a Tidewater Virginia family of landed gentry of English cavalier ancestry.

Ellen Glasgow Home

Francis Glasgow's great – grandfather Arthur came from Ulster to the U.S. with his two brothers Robert and Joseph in 1766. The family settled on the James River in the wilderness of Rockbridge County and they named their substantial Plantation of 4000-5000 acres, 'Green Forest'- which they understood to be the original meaning of the name 'Glasgow'. Their motto was, 'Let Glasgow flourish' and indeed this is what happened because they became the largest land- holders in Rockbridge County.

Francis was successful as a business man and rose to become Managing Director of Tredegar Iron Works in Richmond Virginia. The firm was renowned as the largest supplier of ordnance and munitions during The Civil War. Francis worked tirelessly there until he retired aged 82 in 1912.In human terms however Ellen felt that her father lacked compassion and that not only was his manner at home domineering, but that he displayed an unforgiving form of

Calvinism in his attitude to others. She characterised Francis as stern and emotionally distant to the extent that his personality took a serious toll on the family. To Ellen's way of thinking, as Francis got older so he became increasingly taciturn and withdrew to within his puritanical beliefs and psyche. As evidence of his strict personality she quoted his favourite hymn as being one which bore the line, 'there is a fountain filled with blood'. Ironically this stern outlook of Francis Glasgow's, at least as his daughter perceived it, is a recurring theme in her novels which often portray a bullying father abusing his authority within the family unit.

On the other hand she described her mother as a, 'laughing spirit' and as, 'a perfect flower of the Tidewater in Virginia'. Ellen felt that her father neither understood nor appreciated her mother. Anne Glasgow had survived 10 childbirths and the strain of living in Richmond during its significant role in The Civil War. She was somewhat prone to bouts of depression and nervous exhaustion. When Anne died in 1893 Ellen was then just 20 years of age and believed that Francis had contributed negatively to her mother's debilitation. She found herself to be very much at odds with her father and his outlook on life. Later she also believed that Francis had been insensitive in his treatment of her brother Frank and that this had been a contributory factor in the latter's suicide in 1909.

It is somewhat ironical that Ellen Glasgow's focus on her father's personality, and her heightened powers of concentration, may have prompted the creation of so many excellent novels. Her compulsion to focus in this way may also have resulted from a tendency to overcompensate as a result of her profound deafness. As a result Ellen was largely educated at home. She didn't mix with other school friends of her age but instead read widely of her own volition and choosing.

Ellen Glasgow

Arguably this same set of life experiences and consequences may also have helped to shape Ellen Glasgow's political ideas.

Before she was 20 years of age Ellen Glasgow had read, and been much influenced by, a book entitled 'Progress and Poverty' by a political writer named Henry George. This led to her espousal of a form of Fabian Socialism which was 'left of centre' but opposed to the concept of Revolution. She believed that in the post Civil- War era whatever enemies the people of

The South felt that they had, their real enemies were the same as those of the rest of Mankind namely, 'cruelty, greed and intolerance'. The enemy of the Southern white community, which was often Scots Irish in origin, was not the Northern states nor people of other ethnic origin but rather the 'enemy within'. And yet so much of Ellen Glasgow's consciousness was associated with , 'the Old South', to which her ties were strong. This dichotomy is well summed up in her words, 'all change is not growth, as all movement is not forward'. All of this thinking shaped the characters and plots of her novels.

Largely as a result of her deafness Ellen Glasgow found romantic relationships to be difficult. As she put it in her autobiography, 'at twenty two, I told myself that marriage was not for me.' That was indeed to be the case. However romantic 'love' itself was to be a significant part of her life. In 1899 Ellen returned from a trip abroad having met a man in New York with whom she had become romantically involved, even though he was already married. She referred to him in her autobiography as simply, 'Gerald B….'.It is clear that Ellen felt empowered by the relationship almost to the point where she forgot about her deafness. Gerald died in 1905 and it was not until 12 years later that she became engaged to Henry W. Anderson but this did not last and their engagement was eventually broken off.

Ellen Glasgow wrote twenty novels, all of which portrayed the Scots Irish in Virginia either as the protagonists or minor characters. Her novels engaged seriously with issues of race, class and gender in a way that many southern writers, who sentimentalized Southern society, completely avoided. In this, 'brave new world' deliverance is achieved through love and acceptance and social standing is no longer a matter of, 'good breeding'. The Pulitzer Prize was awarded in 1942 for, 'A Certain Measure', her novel of the previous year.

Notwithstanding such awards Ellen Glasgow believed that her 1935 novel, 'Vein of Iron' was her best work. The novel concerns the fortunes of the Scots-Irish family of Adam Fincastle and in particular the part played by the strong women of the family in Virginia in the early part of the twentieth century. Ellen Glasgow's biographer Susan Goodman has said that whatever differences Ellen Glasgow may have had with her father, "she reluctantly linked his Scotch-Irish heritage with the fortitude or 'vein of iron' she thought necessary for survival." The novel tells the story with considerable depth of character and plot.

Ellen Glasgow died of heart disease at her Virginia home on November 21st 1945 and was buried in the Hollywood Cemetery in Richmond.

Of all the many quotations attributed to Ellen Glasgow there is one which more than any other sums up her approach to life:

"Women are one of the Almighty's enigmas to prove to men that He knows more than they do."

23

The Legendary Dinsmoor Family

In 1828 Robert Dinsmoor published his volume, 'Incidental Poems' and with it a Preface which contained an autobiographical sketch of his life. This has proved to be a useful source for the detail of his and his family's Ulster Scots origins...

'My father's great grandfather was an emigrant from a place in Scotland, called Achenmead, near the river Tweed, and was the only one of the name who ever settled in Ireland from that country. He took his residence in or near Ballywattick, I think in the county of Antrim, and I have been informed lately by a nephew of Colonel Means, who left that country not long since, that a number of Dinsmoors live there to this day.' In a recent telephone conversation with the author, Mr William Dinsmoor a descendant today living at 'Achenmead Farm' Gortin Road, Kilrea, Co. Londonderry confirmed these details and added that Dinsmoor Family story has it that his ancestor John Dinsmoor left Scotland because he was unwilling to hold the stirrup for his elder brother, the laird of Achenmead, to enable him to ostentatiously mount his horse. True or false the story says something about the independence of these Ulster Scots and their unwillingness to be placed in a servile position. The townland of Ballywattick lies on the edge of Ballymoney in the direction of Coleraine, quite close to Ballycormick and Seacon. The Hearthmoney and Subsidy Rolls show John Dinsmoor listed as living at Ballywattick in 1666 and we know that it was here that his son John was born in 1671. It was the latter who emigrated to New England in the early 1720's, not long after the exodus of Rev. McGregor of Macosquin, and the 'five ships' which carried most of his congregation to New England. Like many of these settlers Dinsmoor settled in Maine before moving to the Londonderry New Hampshire region.

Robert Dinsmoor's autobiographical sketch tells us that John settled first in Maine at the English Fort George. He built a house and enjoyed good relationships with the local Indians and quoted how his Native American neighbours told him that they were, 'all one brother.' This was the situation as it pertained just before the war between Great Britain and France which is sometimes known as Lovell's War. One day, 'Daddy Dinsmoor,' as he became known was shingling his house when whooping Indians surrounded his house, ordered him to come down, and told him, 'no longer one brother, you go Canada.' He was taken prisoner and held in captivity for three months. The chief's name was also John and 'Daddy Dinsmoor' became his 'manservant' and as such these two became friends. One day during the chief's absence John Dinsmoor was accused of 'spying' for British authorities in the vicinity. For this crime he was sentenced to be burnt at the stake and was physically in this position when the chief returned and ordered that he be cut free until an enquiry could be held. This consisted of an examination of footprints and luckily it exonerated 'Daddy Dinsmoor' whom the chief then released with basic survival rations and advised him to take refuge in Boston. John Dinsmoor made his way back to Fort George and from there to Boston. From Boston he headed for The Scots Irish settlement of Londonderry New Hampshire where he was generally well-known. Many of the inhabitants of the town had known 'Daddy Dinsmoor' back in Ireland and had a high regard for him. They were much moved by his plight and the proprietors of Londonderry made him a gift of 100 acres of excellent land and confirmed it by deed to him and his heirs forever. John Dinsmoor was a stonemason by trade and built for himself a stone house. He then sent to Ireland for his wife and children to join him, as well as the children born to him by his first wife. In May 1731 William, the father of Robert the poet, was born and shortly after that came Samuel who was throughout his life much esteemed by his elder brother. 'Daddy Dinsmoor' lived for another ten years after William was born and built many houses in the town. Some have speculated that his 'kidnap' experience led to his building a large number of stone houses which provided the townspeople of Londonderry with a greater sense of security during the French and Indian war. Robert Dinsmoor built his own house in that part of Londonderry which was known as Windham. This area was later to be constituted as a municipality in its own right.

It was here on October 7th 1757 that the 'Rustic Poet', Robert Dinsmoor was born. Robert did not attend school until he was 9 years old and then his teacher was one Master McKeen. He fought at the Battle of Saratoga when he was just 20 years of age and soon after married his childhood sweetheart Molly Park and settled down to farm in Windham. Before he was 30 years of age Robert Dinsmoor had become an elder in the church and throughout his life was a zealous defender of the Presbyterian faith, including in his verse, as will be seen later in this account.

His poetry was much favoured by the great Massachusetts Quaker poet John Greenleaf Whittier who summed up his life in these well-chosen words:

'He lived to a good old age, a home loving, unpretending farmer, cultivating his acres with his own horny hands, and cheering the long rainy days and winter evenings with homely rhyme. Most of his pieces were written in the dialect of his ancestors, which was well understood by his neighbours and friends, the only audience upon which he could venture to calculate, he loved all old things, old language, old customs, old theology........... He wrote sometimes to amuse his neighbours, often to soothe their sorrow under domestic calamity, or to give expression to his own.'

His poetry came to him quite naturally and is chocked full of sentiment and the Doric humour that is associated with the Scots tongue. As with Burns, the 'Rustic Poet' was not afraid to deal with life's little everyday problems in all their gory detail. So an unfortunate and potentially embarrassing temporary illness is described thus:

'With senna, salts and castor oil,
They drenched me every little while;
The strong disease such power could foil,
To yield full loth;
At length we found the foe recoil,
At the hot bath.'

Dinsmoor's Presbyterian anti-establishment view of aristocratic and Episcopal power back in the land of his grandfather comes across strongly in his verse in, 'The Poet's Farewell To The Muses', which runs as follows:

'And where our fathers long had been
By lords and bishops pressed.
His rhyme then did chime then
Like music through my heart.'

Such was the range of his poetic pitch that Dinsmoor's verse was also capable of expressing tenderness as in the lines which he wrote in the Autumn of his beloved Molly's death. These lines also create an incidental vignette which allows the reader a sight of the linen production which was brought to Londonderry New Hampshire by the original Ulster Scots who built the town:

' No more I'll wander there alone,
And lean upon the mossy stone,
Where once she piled her wood.
'Twas there she bleached her linen cloth'
By yonder bass-wood tree;'

As you might expect matters theological were often written about in his rhymes, sometimes humorously as in 'Springs Lament', which described a dog interrupting a sermon, and sometimes more seriously as when he advised Rev. McGregor's son David, who was also a Presbyterian Minister, as to how to defend his faith in the face of Unitarian attack:

'When Unitarian champions dare thee,
Goliah like, and think to scare thee.
Dear Davie, fear not, they'll ne'er waur thee;
But draw thy sling,
Weel loaded frae the Gospel quarry,
An gi'et a fling.'

Robert Dinsmoor's brother Samuel also achieved distinction in his contribution to life in America in so far as he was a graduate of Dartmouth College and married a daughter of General Reid of Revolutionary fame, became a member of Congress and Governor of New Hampshire. His son, another Samuel, followed his father and also became Governor of New Hampshire. Margaret, a sister of Robert and Samuel senior married Deacon Samuel Morrison and their grandson Leonard Morrison served in both houses of the New Hampshire

Legislature and was the author of, 'The History of The Dinsmoor Family in Scotland, Ireland and America.'

In time other members of the Dinsmoor family were to make their mark across America with some members of the family changing the spelling of the name to Dinsmore. So today we can find towns bearing this name in Arkansas, California, Florida, Missouri, Mississippi, Pennsylvania, and Texas.

Two of the core elements that interest people in Scots Irish culture and history are the creativity of the original 'Lallans' Lowland Scots vocabulary and the vitality of the Scots Irish in their contribution to the building of America. Quite uniquely the Dinsmoor story brings these two elements together as one.

Daniel Dinsmoor

24

Horace Greeley - Conscience of America

Horace Greeley was born in Amherst, New Hampshire on February 3rd 1811. He was the third of seven children. His father Zaccheus Greeley's family was of English derivation having originally arrived in New England from Nottinghamshire in 1650. As one biographer has put it his mother Mary Woodburn, who was from Londonderry New Hampshire was, 'of that fine old Scotch-Irish stock which settled the town.' Indeed the Woodburn family had emigrated from the Garvagh area of Co Londonderry in 1718. Members of the Woodburn Family had been present at the great Siege of Derry, as Horace Greeley was well aware and indeed wrote about in later life. The Greeley and Woodburn farms were virtually adjoining and so it was not all that remarkable when in 1807 Zaccheus and Mary were married. Although they had no inheritance they managed to scrape enough cash together to buy the Amherst farm where Horace and his siblings were born. On the farm the young Horace performed his fair share of

Horace Greeley's birthplace and Marker

chores including, 'riding the horse to plough' and 'picking stones'.

The Scots Irish settlers of Londonderry had brought their linen manufacturing skills with them from Ulster and indeed were renowned for their 'Londonderry Linen'. Horace Greeley had an abiding memory of his mother seated at her spinning wheel and regaling the children with an inexhaustible repertoire of songs, ballads and stories to which the boy listened greedily

As was so often the case Scots Irish work skills and culture were closely associated with each other. Horace Greeley, in his autobiography, would later fondly recall these pieces and commented that, 'they served to awaken in me a thirst for knowledge, and a lively interest in learning and history.' Horace benefited from his mother's nurture and could read children's books by the age of 3 years old and adult books by the time he reached 4 years of age. After this time the family moved from place to place around New England and Horace continued to read avidly both the newspaper which came into the house, 'The Farmer's Cabinet' and books which he bought for himself with pocket money earned from his industrious hobbies such as, 'bee-hunting and nut picking.'

When Horace was fifteen he noticed an advert in The Northern Spectator for a 'boy wanted' for its own office in Poultney and his father reluctantly allowed him to begin an

Horace Greeley House

Horace Greeley

Horace Greeley reading

apprenticeship with the paper which would last from April 18th 1826 until he was 20 years old. The work was hard and back-breaking as operating a heavy press was too much for the boy's light frame. However the job did permit Horace time for reading and this he put to good use. In the town debating society's competitions he inevitably triumphed as a result of very extensive reading and a good memory. He was a fluent speaker and never lost his temper. However in June 1830, The Northern Spectator wound up its operation and Horace Greeley moved first to Sodus New York and then to Erie Pennsylvania where he obtained printing jobs. By now he was also providing journalistic input to papers. By 1831 he was living and working in New York City. At this time he also adopted the Universalistic religious ideology and worshipped initially at Orchard Street

Universalist Church and later at the Universalist Church on Broadway in the city. In New York he worked initially on various papers until in 1834 he started a steady position with The New Yorker for which he held sole editorial responsibility for the next 7 years. In 1841 he started The New York Tribune, with 600 subscribers and borrowed capital of £1000. This publication was one of the first 'penny dailies' and became a very influential newspaper. It didn't offer its readers any sensationalism but instead concentrated on regular features and book reviews. The paper took a clear moral stance and spoke out against capital punishment, the Mexican War, and in particular Slavery. By 1856 Horace Greeley had not only published a number of books, including one which was a comprehensive denunciation of Slavery, but he had also entered The House of Representatives for a brief session and travelled extensively in

Horace Greeley Statue - City Hall, New York City. In front of Pace University

Horace Greeley postage stamp, 1961

Europe. Also by now The Tribune was on a high road to success and recorded annual profits in the region of $30,000. In this year Greeley also helped found the new Republican Party. He also wrote and spoke eloquently in advocating reform in a great number of spheres, supporting temperance, transcendentalism, and labour unions. He possessed an ability to express idealistic and moral opinions in prose that was clear and easily remembered. To him is attributed the phrase, 'Go west young man!' Under his management the Tribune was the first national newspaper to be distributed by rail and steamboat. The paper is accredited with having united the people behind his moderate anti-slavery approach. As an early member of The Republican Party Greeley helped secure the party's nomination of Abraham Lincoln as its Presidential candidate in 1860. He was later to be quite critical of Lincoln for not releasing the slaves promptly.

Greeley was himself to later run for the office of President against Ulysses Simpson Grant. In 1872 Horace Greeley received the nomination of The Liberal Republican Party and indeed The Democratic Party also supported his candidature. Greeley opposed Grant because he believed in 'one term

Horace Greeley Statue, Greeley Square, between 32nd and 33rd Street, Manhattan, New York City

candidature' and that the Civil Service needed major reform if it was to overcome, 'arbitrary favouritism and patronage' .Surprisingly his manifesto also recommended that Jefferson Davis the President of the now defeated Confederacy should be released from prison in order to improve relations with the South. Criticism of Greeley the Presidential candidate was fierce and he found the cartoons of Thomas Nast to be particularly wounding. Nast was a German immigrant and so influential were these cartoons, which were equivalent I suppose to electioneering television adverts of today, that many considered him to be, 'The President Maker'. Horace Greeley said at the time that the criticism was so toxic that he sometimes wondered whether, 'he was running for the Presidency or the Penitentiary'. By 1872 the days of personal editorial autonomy had passed and not only did Horace Greeley lose the election but also the editorship of the Tribune passed out of his hands. The result of this double blow was to cause Horace Greeley to have a complete breakdown of body and mind and he died shortly afterwards on November 29th 1872, just a few weeks after the election.

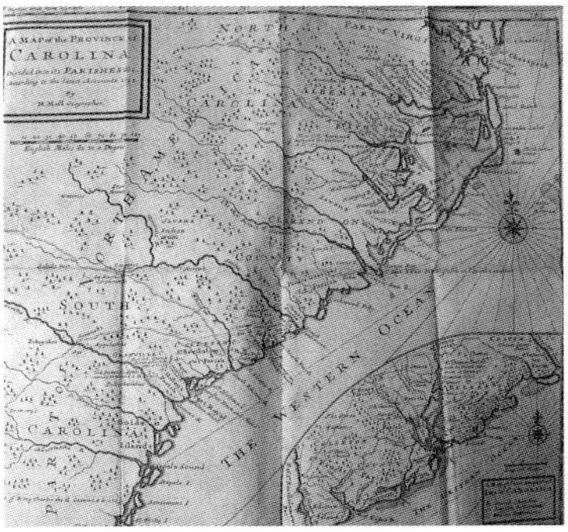

25

George Galphin and The Rea Brothers - Challenging the Stereotype - Defying Hagiography - Scots Irish Settlement in Georgia

To say that neither George Galphin nor The Rea brothers fit the stereotypical paradigm of the Calvinist God-fearing Scots Irish emigrant is something of an understatement .Of the two parties George Galphin's exploits present the more outrageous litany and includes, bigamy, fathering 9 illegitimate children with 4 different mothers of diverse racial background as well as dealing in slaves and rum and particularly using the latter to 'subdue' members of the Creek Indian tribes of Georgia. While his business partner John Rea did not quite match this record his method of obtaining Indian land by exploiting contrived circumstances and a charge of manslaughter somewhat stained his record.

All of this is not to say that either man did not achieve anything positive in their lives-quite the contrary as this chapter will seek to uncover… Their story is quite remarkable..

The Rea Brothers in Ireland

It is believed that this particular branch of the Rea family originated in Bromfield Parish near Wigton in Cumberland. Wills are recorded for the family existing there from 1578 onwards. In 1676 Isabel Rea gave to Elizabeth Grainger her best coat, shift, and waistcoat. John Grainger was left some household goods in this same bequest. David Rea, who is the starting point for the Ulster Rea family, and who lived from 1672 until 1754, in his will to his wife Debra, bequeathed to her amongst other possessions all land belonging to him , 'that were in the possession of John and Robert Grainger.' David Rea may have been born in the Killeen, Holywood Co. Down area and subsequently moved to live at Ballycreen, Magheraknock area near Ballynahinch Co.Down. Although a Presbyterian by religious persuasion he is buried as is often the custom in Ulster in the Church of Ireland graveyard in Saintfield Co. Down. John Rea, the main member of the family portrayed in this paper was a son of David and was baptized in Ballynahinch Presbyterian Church on April 16th 1710. Earlier in July 1705 a child with the same name and a son of David's is recorded as having been baptized and the assumption may be made that this child died in infancy and as was often the case this later child was named in his memory. The Ballycreen home was a farm and the family also ran a mill at Magheraknock which was held from the Annesley family. Other children from David's first marriage included John's business partner brother Matthew, although the baptismal records don't give his date but this is believed to have been around 1713.

The exact date of John Rea's emigration is not known but it is clear that his son John was born in Fort Moore (now Augusta) Georgia in 1740. Matthew was living at Drumbo near Lisburn in the Lagan Valley by 1765 where the Rea family continued to hold land until about a hundred years later. There was no ambiguity about his base there as it was, 'a fact he stated in all his advertisements.'

George Galphin in Ireland

George Galphin was born in 'Tullamore' County Armagh in the early 1700's (possibly 1709) and this is probably the area known today as 'Tullymore' and is within the boundary of the ancient city of Armagh itself. His father was Thomas Galphin a linen weaver and his mother's name was Barbara (nee Rankin). On 28th September 1736 he married Catherine Saunderson of Enniskillen but in the following year he is seen entering the port of Charlestown as a poor immigrant and alone. He had left behind not just his new wife but also a younger brother, four younger sisters and his widowed mother.

Development of the Emigration business

After 1763 when the Peace of Paris brought the Spanish threat to Georgia's borders to an end John Rea developed a scheme to colonize Ulster Protestant settlers in the empty lands along the Ogeechee River about forty miles south west of Augusta on the South Carolina border. In the period 1764-5 Rea and Galphin obtained land grants totalling 80,000 acres along Lamberts Creek which was situated just across the Ogeechee from Indian Territory. John Rea wrote to his brother Matthew setting out a glowing prospect for Ulster colonists. Settlers would have little to pay for fertile soils and 100 acres of land would automatically go to the head of a family and 50 acres to every child of whatever size or age. The reciprocation was to be an indenture process whereby individuals would pay for their passage by working for 4 years of service starting immediately they arrived.

In return they would receive £5.00 annually and their, 'bed and board', as well as the prospect of a £4.00 bonus and lands as above. Matthew, living at Drumbo, advertised all of this on behalf of his brother John. He added as a further inducement the free use of cows and horses for 5 years. This advertisement appeared in The Belfast Newsletter in 1763 in preparation for the land bounty that the Rea brothers and George Galphin felt would be theirs very soon. In 1761 Rea and 10 others had petitioned South Carolina for a grant of 40,000 acres to be used for building townships for Ulster settlers. This did not materialise but Rea and Galphin were not to be outdone and made similar approaches in Georgia.

When the Creeks ceded land to Georgia between the Savannah and Ogeechee rivers the Governor James Wright was eager to attract settlers. Rea and Galphin petitioned Georgia for a bounty to cover passage, settlement and a 10 year exemption from any tax or rent. George Galphin purchased 1500 acres on the Ogeechee River at the edge of Indian territory. Here he established a herd of cattle and a trading post. He called the site, 'Galphin's Old Town'. The Bill covering the immigration project passed through the Georgia Assembly in February 1764 and opened settlement to Protestant families who arrived in groups of 40 or more during the next 3 years. The advertisement inviting settlers to come from Ulster asked them to sign up with Mr Robert Pooler and advised that the port of exit would be either Belfast or Newry and the port of entry was to be Charlestown. John Rea may well have believed that the project would be successful given the number of similar settlers pouring into neighbouring South Carolina but the Act emerging out of the 1764 Georgia Bill was disallowed by the Westminster Government on the grounds that it might have a debilitating effect on Ulster if too many of its Protestant citizens took ship for the Colonies. The feeling was that the process would weaken the ongoing strategy of deliberately 'planting' British settlers in Catholic Ulster and would draw merchants and craftsmen from the Ulster economy. However 4 ships were commissioned to carry emigrants to the New World. These were, The Prince George, The Hopewell (2 trips), The Two Peggies, and the Britannia. Two other ships brought some emigrants to the settlement- The Waddell and The Elizabeth. Two or more of these ships went first to Philadelphia and then south to Charleston South Carolina (the present day Boonsboro settlement) and from there to Savannah Georgia.

Settlers began to arrive in 1768 and Governor Wright of Georgia designated their land as Queensborough. By that year Galphin was describing the venture as a, 'growing and flourishing province, where industry is amply rewarded.' The resettlement now cost 1 guinea (21 shillings) per passenger but a standard plot of 100 acres was tax free for 10 years and Galphin's promise still stood to supply each head of household with milk cows and horses until such time as they could afford their own. John Rea's advert in The Belfast Newsletter of that year sought 200 people who might be keen to come to Queensborough.By June 1768 some 26 settlers had registered individual grants. A group of emigrants boarding The Hopewell in December 1769 plainly stated that the taxes in Ireland were so high that even the best jobs could not support a sufficient standard of living.

The Queensborough settlement became problematic due in part to its location which was as stated adjacent to Indian Territory. The Creeks had no compunction about crossing settlers' lands. This may have been contrary to Euro /American convention but, as with many aboriginal people throughout the world, the Creeks had scant understanding of the concept of private ownership.

They also stole livestock and Rea and Galphin were anxious to contain the tensions that inevitably arose out of contact at these interfaces. In December 1771 a Creek killed a settler called John Cary and

Galphin himself with a posse of his slaves tracked the assailant and handed him over to the Creeks who executed him in front of the traders.

In any case only about 95 families (250 people) settled on John Rea's 20,000 acres since only 25% of the potential land was released by the Georgia authorities. By 1775 only 70 families lived in Queensborough itself and perhaps another 200 lived in the environs of the town. From the Georgian authorities point of view the situation was not totally negative in that about 1000 emigrants came to Savannah in the voyages made by the aforementioned ships. Between 1760 and 1770 the colony's white population rose from around 9,000 to more than 25,000 and to some extent due to overspill for the continuing South Carolina projects the 'white' population of Georgia had risen to 82,500 by 1790.

Rea Brothers' position in society in Georgia

By 1751, about 20 years after he became a resident of Georgia John Rea had been appointed as a Conservator of the Peace. Four years later in 1755 he was elected as a Representative to sit in the Assembly for Georgia which met in Augusta. In 1771 John Rea was convicted of the manslaughter of Mrs Ann Simpson of Savannah but evidence suggests that he was later pardoned. His friends petitioned on his behalf stating that he had been in Georgia for several decades with an unblemished record and had held several positions of public trust including having been a highly esteemed member of The Georgia Assembly.

John Rea died in Richmond County in 1784 and left extensive real estate holdings in Augusta. Mary Osborne surmises that, 'his early life on the farm in Ballynahinch had prepared him for land management tasks'. His main Plantation, Rea's Hall was 5 miles from Savannah and he owned land in Augusta, on Hutchinson's Island and various city lots in Savannah itself. He had a record as a Patriot, having served in The Revolutionary War as did his two sons-in-law, General Samuel Elbert and Colonel Joseph Habersham, both of whom became Governors of Georgia. Rea's Hall was built on Yamacraw Indian land and later archaeological excavation revealed that the Rea's kinsfolk were interred there including General Elbert himself. John Rea's business partner George Galphin played a very significant role in Georgia life, particularly in The Revolutionary War. His record in the Province however is riddled with controversy, much of it the product of his flamboyant personality.

George Galphin-Personal Life

When Galphin emigrated in 1737 he left behind his young wife Catherine Saunderson to whom he had been married for less than a year. Notwithstanding this and without any legal separation or divorce he married again to Bridget Shaw shortly after his arrival in St Philips Church Charleston South Carolina. He subsequently fathered 9 children by white, black and Creek mothers By 1745 South Carolina authorities were deploying George Galphin as an interpreter. His first post in this role was among the Lower Creeks around the Flint and Chattahoochee rivers.

Part of the brief as well as being an interpreter was to keep the government well informed about Creek activity.

Relatively early in his career his service proved to be of an ilk that was not always above reproach. He presented a bill to the South Carolina Assembly for £467.00 for Indian trade goods. The Assembly body found that this included overestimates of £114.00. The Assembly also found that he spent £83.00 to supply the Creeks with rum.

Galphin's conscience may have been pricked in later life as is shown by his will, which left "50 pounds sterling to be shared among the poor of Eneskilling and 50 pounds sterling to be shared among the poor of Amagh (*sic*) in Ireland."

His various children were remembered in his will. Those children born of Metawney an Indian princess of the Coweta Tyger clan of Creeks were given land and to Creek Nitechuckey's daughter Rose was given her freedom.

Thus it may be concluded that Galphin had retained his own offspring as slaves.

His only 'white' offspring were born to a French girl named Rachel Dupee and a date is recorded for Martha, sister of Thomas, to the effect that she was born in 1764.

Martha later married John Milledge who became governor of Georgia. Interestingly both Galphin and John Rea were thus to have sons-in-law who became Governors of the Province.

In the 1740s Galphin joined the Augusta-based trading firm of Brown, Rea and Company. This firm had been established earlier by Archibald Gillivray who was the ancestor of Galphin's friend and colleague Lachlan Gillivray.

This company employed about twenty packhorse men and owned 123 horses. Since 1741 the firm had been controlled by Patrick Brown who was licensed to trade with the Upper Creek towns and John Rea and George Galphin brought to this venture their licence to trade with the Lower Creeks.

In this operation George Galphin was renounced for extending so much credit to Creeks that they were forced to cede land to the government to pay their bills.

The government then often sold the land to the traders.

When there was a problem or hitch in this operation Brown, Rea and Company – the powerful 'gentlemen of Augusta' wrote to John Stuart the Superintendent of Indian Affairs to make the point that unless problems were eased the traders would leave the back country and leave the Indians undersupplied.

Stuart was the representative of the British authorities to the indigenous tribes. His role was either to keep the Indians peaceful or to stir them up to oppose Britain's enemies.

The key to this process lay with the trade goods. This provided a context inside which contact could take place. Without the context there could be no contact process.

One Brown and Rea scheme requested the British Government to sell ceded lands to Virginians – many of whom were Scots Irish in origin.

The scale of tobacco production and the need for wide open space for tobacco growing and processing had pushed many of these people out of their farms. Galphin worked to ensure the co-operation of the Creeks in this matter and received funds from Government sales of this land that amounted to £9,971. Galphin however never lived to see this money 'in his hand' since the area came under loyalist control and Galphin was branded guilty of high treason for his work in support of the patriot Cause. His heirs were denied the monies also until the matter was settled in their favour in an 1850 lawsuit which saw an award of $191,000 being made.

Galphin's role was not easy as far as the settlers were concerned either. In order to protect themselves from the Creeks, who weren't singularly happy about this 'Virginian' settlement or indeed the settlement of people coming directly from Ulster, the Scots Irish decided on 'vigilante' activity and the Creeks retaliated to this by carrying out killings amongst the settlers in 1773.

At this the Government ordered a trade embargo but George Galphin did not comply with this instruction. Resentment about his role was already building up by the outbreak of the American Revolution.

John Stuart was ordered to mobilise the Indians on behalf of the British cause. The initial problem for George Galphin arose in December 1775 when Stuart notified the Secretary of State that the Continental Congress had named three former traders to act as Superintendents for the Patriot cause in the Georgia area. These officials were named as Galphin, Edward Wilkinson and John Rea – i.e. the firm of Brown, Rea and Co.

Galphin informed Congress, through his representative Henry Laurens, that the American cause would be best served by keeping the Creeks peaceable through ensuring that trade was kept going. He further added that this would help them to keep faith in his position and enable him to keep their confidence.

Laurens replied on Feb 14th 1776 and drew attention to the recent supply of gunpowder which he had sent him with which to supply the Creeks and he encouraged Galphin to make sure that the Creeks received whatever rum and other goods he could muster.

In September 1775 Galphin is reported as having told the Creeks that the patriots were fighting against the 'great king' who wanted to stop their trade. He worked hard to keep the Creeks loyal to the patriots. There were anti-Indian groups on his own side which made his work difficult.

He wrote again to Henry Laurens in July 1777 complaining that were it not "...for those damed *(sic)* villains upon the frontier I should tacke *(sic)* pleasure in serving my country."

There is some evidence to suggest that Galphin was making himself such a 'thorn in the flesh' that Stuart funded an assassination attempt on him in the fall of 1777. In what was a case of mistaken identity Captain John Gerard was killed instead of Galphin.

Certainly for a period George Galphin exercised tremendous control over the Indians even though his life was endangered.

Henry Laurens urged all patriots to pray for George Galphin's continued good health and safety from being killed. Galphin operated in such a way that if he couldn't keep the peace then he devised factions to work against each other. He persuaded the Creeks under their chief, 'Handsome Fellow' to attack loyalist subjects and drive them from the Georgia backcountry.

Unfortunately Galphin's influence was tied to trade and the goods which the Creeks bought. When the supply of goods dried up the Creeks attacked and killed "numerous Georgian citizens of Queensborough."

Patriot officials ordered George Galphin to cut off all supplies in retaliation, so he found himself in an invidious situation with both Indians and settlers threatening to kill him. This position was further eroded when the British allegedly found letters from Galphin to the Creeks urging general rebellion against the Crown authorities.

In 1778, about 90 of Galphin's slaves left his estate and joined Lieutenant Campbell's forces since Britain offered freedom to any slaves who joined their cause.

George Galphin died at Silver Bluff, South Carolina on December 1st 1788.

Since many of the Queensborough settlers were loyalists the patriot visitors confiscated their estates and the name

Queensborough was renounced as being too Pro-British. In a sense Rea and Galphin's ventures and successes were both made and broken by the circumstances around the American Revolution.

By 1790 the white population of Georgia was 82,500 and Galphin in particular was remembered for the crucial 'dirty war' role he had played during the Revolutionary period.

John Milledge, Galphin's son-in-law.

Londonderry Presbyterian Church

26

THE SCOTS IRISH IN NEW ENGLAND

THE amount of Scots Irish blood that flows in the veins of the people of New England is often underestimated. Indeed several cities and towns in New England were entirely founded by Ulster immigrants. One commentator has reckoned that between 1714 and 1720, 54 shiploads of Scots Irish arrived at Boston Harbour. One very significant flotilla in this Diaspora occurred in 1718 when five ships full of Ulster Presbyterian emigrants landed in Boston Massachusetts under the leadership of their Minister, Rev. James McGregor. This particular group of migrants were not made at all welcome by the Puritan fathers of the city. Nonetheless some of these Ulster folk decided to 'stay put' in Boston. Almost immediately they were threatened that they would be placed on the 'tax roll' and 'woe betide them' if they couldn't pay the amount required by the Puritan burghers of the City.

However others in their party, in that late autumn of 1718, moved to Haverhill, Andover and Dracut where they could 'winter over' and establish their 'place' in the American Colonies. After six months had elapsed they had formed into three main settlements consisting of:-

Worcester Massachusetts

Nutfield (later Londonderry) New Hampshire

Casco Bay Maine

As regards the latter group, and the overall number of Scots Irish descendants in Maine, it is essential to note that there were also ships which travelled directly to the coast of Maine. To believe, as some commentators appear to, that the bulk of the Scots Irish in Maine are descended from the 'five ships' is as misleading as it would be to believe that all the Scots living in Ulster in the eighteenth century were descendants of the 'official' 1610 Plantation of Ulster.

In Boston the Scots Irish founded a Presbyterian congregation on Long Lane (later known as Federal Street) under the Rev. John Moorehead. As a result of constant pressure by 1786 this had eventually been converted into a Congregational Church.

The Worcester Scots Irish community of 1718 originally consisted of 50 log cabins and thus 50 families, giving a population of approximately 200 people. At that time they were settled on what was effectively 'the frontier' and were subject to the constant fear of being attacked by Native Americans. Within the Worcester community the Youngs were a particularly interesting family. William Young, who was a stone-cutter, designed and erected a monument to his father who was the patriarch of the community. It bears the following inscription:

"Here lies interred the remains of John Young, who was born in the Isle of Bert (Sic) near Londonderry, in the Kingdom of Ireland. He departed this life June 30, 1730, aged 107 years."

This same family is credited with having introduced the 'Irish potato' into North America. The potato which, years earlier, Sir Walter Raleigh had brought to Europe from America was in fact a 'sweet potato' i.e. a totally different plant.

In Worcester the local Puritans continued to harass and threaten the Scots Irish Presbyterians. In 1710 they actually tore down the Presbyterian Meeting House. Not surprisingly this gave rise to some of the Scots Irish of Worcester being 'on the move again' and they joined kinsfolk in nearby Framingham and Hopkinton. They also formed four new towns namely Colerain (about 50 miles North West of Worcester), Pelham (30 miles west of Worcester) in 1738, Western (now Warren) in Worcester County in 1741 and Blandford in 1741. Undoubtedly the most seminal and significant of the towns from the, "5 ships Dispersal", has been Londonderry New Hampshire. From early on this city performed the role of nodal point or 'distribution centre' for the spread of the Scots Irish people throughout New England.

Londonderry was first settled by that group of Scots Irish who had fled Boston and wintered over 1718/1719 near Portland in Casco Bay Maine. Amongst this group was a young boy named Matthew Thornton, who was to move to Londonderry at a much later stage, and would grow up to become one on the 'signers' of the Declaration of Independence and emerge as one of the most eminent of Americans of all time.

Even though the Thornton family stayed in Maine for a period there were others in their party who were anxious to move on. In April 1719 about twenty of the families in this group moved to Londonderry New Hampshire (then called Nutfield). Within fifteen years this group had grown to 700 Presbyterians of communicant age and status. Most of these Scots Irish settlers had originally emanated from settlements on the east side of the River Bann such as, Coleraine, Ballymoney, Ballymena and Kilrea. Their leader during this period was James McKeen who was the brother-in-law of Rev. McGregor.

Their land at Nutfield was given as a free grant from King William III by way of recompense for the fact they many of their number, such as Rev. Mathew Clark, had suffered inside the Great Siege of Derry in 1688. Unlike many other Scots Irish settlements during the French and Indian Wars Londonderry remained relatively free from attack. Many of its inhabitants believe that this 'peace' was theirs because Rev. McGregor had been at college with Governor Vaudreuil of Quebec and had a lasting friendship with him that reached beyond the politics of the day. Londonderry New Hampshire gave rise to other namesake settlements in Nova Scotia and New England before the American Revolution. Places like Londonderry Nova Scotia and Londonderry Vermont may be seen as 'grandchildren' of Londonderry in Ulster.

At its core the Kennebec Maine settlement consisted of the original Casco Bay families who had names such as Armstrong, Means (from the Clogher Valley), Jameson, Gray, Gyles and a McDonald.

After Dummer's War (also known as Lovell's War) Robert Temple who had fought during the late war at Cork in Maine brought in and settled a further five ships with 200 'new' Scots Irish families.

In 1728 David Dunbar, a former soldier, was appointed as Surveyor General of the King's Woods, "in American and Nova Scotia". His main objective was to produce supplies and resources for the British Navy and to protect, in particular, white pine trees in the forests of Maine and New Hampshire. The white pine was particularly suitable for the construction of ship masts due to the fact that it contained more sap than other trees and this gave it durability and a flexibility which was so important to ships in strong winds on the high seas. Dunbar's objective was that of creating a separate province between the Kennebec and St Croix rivers. In 1729 he outlined plans to rebuild the Pemaquid, Fort that had been destroyed in 1696, and to rename it Fort Frederick. In his letter to the British authorities he mentioned that as well as the existing Scots Irish settlers from Londonderry New Hampshire he also had, “a great many hundred men of those who came lately from Ireland”. He added that these settlers were waiting in Pennsylvania where they had taken refuge from the ill-treatment that they had received in Boston. The plan was to offer each settler between 50 and 100 acres of land. Eventually 15 families of these ‘Dunbar settlers’ put down roots in Maine. He described his customers as being, “originally from North Britain but last from Ireland.”

Shortly after Dunbar’s venture came the efforts of yet another ‘social engineer’ – Samuel Waldo. He earned his living as a wealthy timber trader and ‘mast agent’. Like Dunbar he also was involved with this particularly lucrative line of naval business. Waldo was also interested in the deposits of lime which had recently been uncovered in Maine. In April 1735 he reached agreement with 32 Scots Irish families and 19 families of other European background that, in return for building a house and clearing four acres of forest, they would each receive 100 acres of land. In a letter of 1736 Waldo outlined further plans and claimed that he “expects a great number of Irish Protestants to arrive in these parts in a month or two”. He further reveals that he has, “engaged three ships for that purpose whose passengers your petitioner has contracted with to settle on the land there”.

Within twelve months of writing this epistle he had indeed attracted further 25 – 35 Scots Irish settler families to Maine. By 1753 Waldo’s son Samuel was actively recruiting in Ulster for a new settlement at Stirling within the same state.

No account of the Scots Irish in Maine would be complete without some mention of Belfast Maine. Situated today in

Waldo County it was originally founded in the summer of 1765 by a surveyor named John Mitchell. Once again it was populated with Scots Irish stock from Londonderry New Hampshire. Amongst the early settlers was James Miller originally from Belfast in Ulster and it was he who lobbied for the City to be named after the place where he himself had been born.

Later movements carried Scots Irish settlers to virtually all the towns of Western Massachusetts and also to most of the towns of Vermont. The Scots Irish who settled at Londonderry New Hampshire, who were so central to much of this development, truly believed that, for all the challenges that their new home presented to them, they had God alongside them and that he had settled them in a good place.

In 1869 one of their number wrote a poem to celebrate their good fortune and providential deliverance:-

"Tis the robin's wedding time,
And a breath of plum and cherry
Makes the air of Londonderry
Sweet as Eden in its prime"

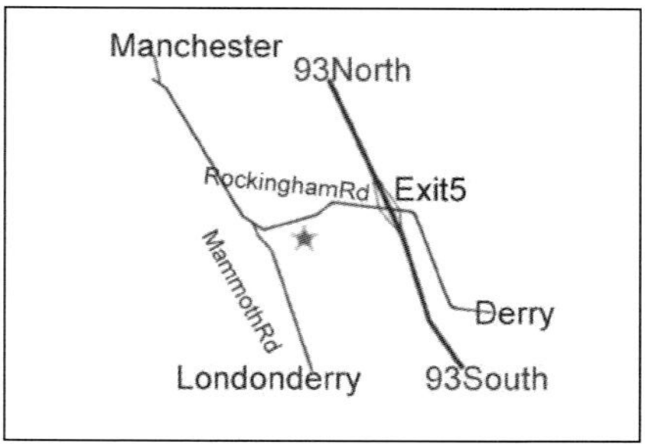

Derry, Londonderry, NH

27

The Scots Irish in Maine

In 1718 five ships sailed from Larne to Boston carrying 120 families from Northern Ireland. Part of the attraction for landing there had been the promise of the free frontier land. In the event the potential settlers were greeted in a fairly hostile manner and fled Boston. Thereafter they split into two groups. One group headed for Worcester on the Western Bay and having been burned out there proceeded to Nutfield (afterwards renamed Londonderry) New Hampshire. The second group sailed to the Eastern frontier and spent a frigid freezing winter on board ship in Casco Bay Maine, close to what is now the town of Portland. Some of this group remained around Falmouth (now Portland) including John Armstrong, Robert Means, William Jameson, Joshua Gray, William Gyles and a McDonald. The majority however fled to join their countrymen at Londonderry New Hampshire – whilst another small group moved east to the shores of Lower Kennebec where they were joined by several hundred Scots Irish immigrants who settled on the shores of Merrymeeting Bay near Bath. Robert Temple brought 5 ships to the Maine shore in 1719 with 200 Scots Irish families and between 1729 and 1731 an Ulster Scot Col. Dunbar moved interrelated clans of Co Tyrone and Co Antrim families from New Hampshire to Maine – largely as a buffer against the Abenaki St Francis Native American allies of the French.

In 1759 an expedition left Portland to capture the mouth of Penobscot from the French. This group included Andrew and Joshua Gray who later settled there. Still living there today are Grays, Wears, Orrs and Doaks with some of these names coming from the original 1718 settlers in Boston.

Other names still traceable today include those who were part of the 1730 Scots Irish who 'resettled' Townsend (Boothbay) - including the Montgomerys of East Boothbay. Others settled in Topsham including the McFadden, McGowen, McConn, Vincent, Hamilton, Johnston, Malcom, McClellan, Crawford, Graves, Ward, Givern, Dunning and Simpson families.

Mowing with oxen, near Belfast, Maine

Main Street, Belfast, Maine

In the past few years there have been a number of accounts of the Scots Irish immigration into the south and south eastern region of the United States. Much less has been written about those Ulster Scots who settled in the 'Wilderness' of the North East.

One commentator has written about the role of this group in the State of Maine as follows – "The history of these people and the impact of their presence in Maine had been relegated to an occasional footnote in the history of the State".

Maine Ulster Scots project has been given the goal of increasing awareness of the Ulster Scots heritage within the State. The project has begun a process of collecting and archiving the histories of Maine's Ulster Scots families.

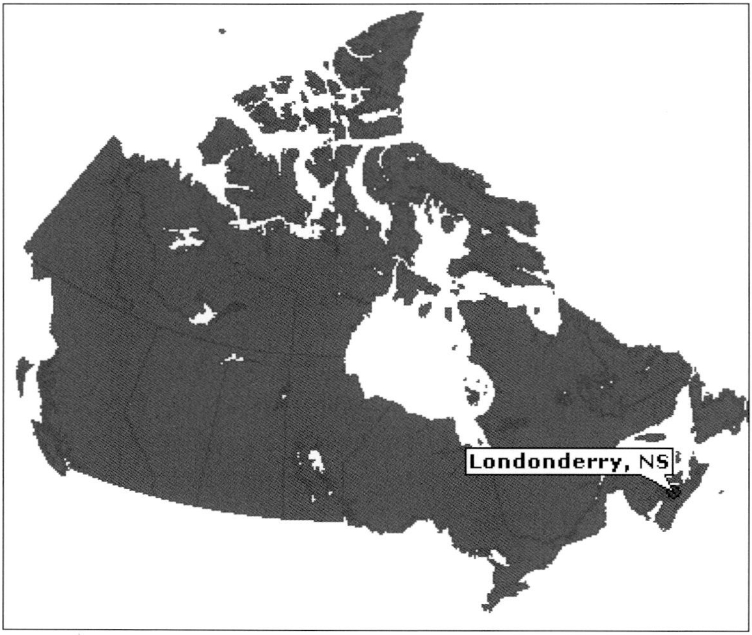

Londonderry, Nova Scotia

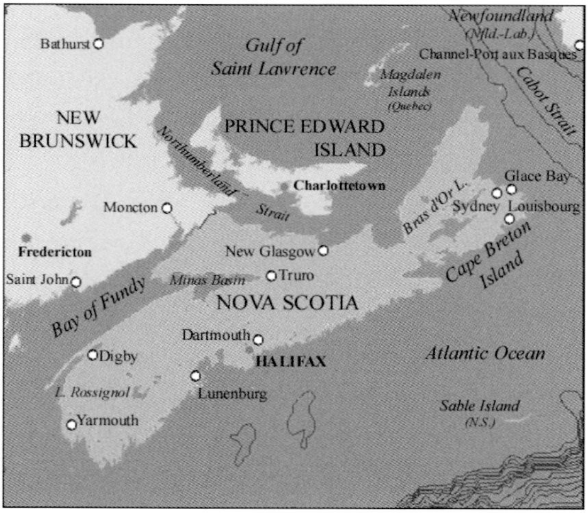

Nova Scotia

28

The Scots Irish in Nova Scotia

Census records show that in 1748 there were 142 French Acadian families living in the Cobequid district of Nova Scotia. In 1755 these people came under sustained pressure from the British authorities and faced with 'Hobson's Choice' they fled from their settlements rather than wait to be forcibly deported. Thereafter their villages were burned to the ground to dissuade the Acadians from ever returning to the region. Subsequently many of these people moved to Louisiana where their name was mispronounced to become 'Cajun' – the nickname which has remained theirs until the present day.

When this process of forced eviction was complete the British authorities published a proclamation in order to attract loyal subjects. The idea was that they would settle this empty space and thus secure the region on behalf of the Crown. Inevitably, as they had in the past, the authorities turned to the Ulster Scots to perform the role that Rory Fitzpatrick has described as 'God's Frontiersmen'. The agent who took on the

Nova Scotia 1896

job of recruiting suitable Ulster Scots settlers for this task was one of their own ilk – Captain Alexander McNutt. This 30 year old son of Londonderry looked first for such people not in his native Ulster (that would happen shortly afterwards) but rather in the areas that the Ulster Scots had settled and made their own 30-40 years earlier – particularly around Londonderry New Hampshire. McNutt himself had lived initially for some time amongst the Scots Irish in Staunton Virginia. Between April and November 1760 McNutt served as a Massachusetts Province Captain at Fort Cumberland near the present day border between Nova Scotia and New Brunswick. This may be how he came to know the area although it is likely that McNutt may have become involved in the 'Nova Scotia Ulster Scots' colonization process because he initially worked for Thomas Hancock who was the Boston agent of Charles Lawrence – the Governor of Nova Scotia. Whatever his motivation McNutt recruited an initial band of 50 'second generation' Scots Irish settlers from New Hampshire who arrived in the Cobequid/Truro area in the Spring of 1761.

McNutt had big plans. He proposed to settle 7-8 thousand 'Protestant Irish' in Nova Scotia. The London Board of Trade accepted the concept but the Privy Council of the day baulked at the scheme as they felt that such a haemorrhage would harm British interests in Ireland. Not completely deterred by this restriction McNutt returned to his native Ulster seeking emigrants. In the Spring of 1761 he advertised throughout Ulster for "industrious farmers and useful mechanics". He offered 200 acres of land to the head of the family and 50 additional acres to each member of the family. This campaign resulted in 300 Ulster colonists on board the 'Hopewell' and the 'Nancy' arriving in Halifax from Londonderry in October of that same year. The original plan was that these people should

Alexander McNutt's Headstone

be set down on the lands which had been afforded for 'planting' on the Northern shores' of the Minas Basin. However it was October – late in the year and they were kept in Halifax to spend the winter where they were supported by both Government and private charity. These immigrants were viewed as being less 'advanced' that the earlier New Hampshire second generation Ulster Scots and were described as being "indigent people".

In the Spring of 1762 the Council of Nova Scotia supplied the settlers with provisions such as seed corn, tools, building materials and a vessel to take them to the Cobequid area. Here they founded Londonderry on the Great Village River in present day Colchester County.

On August 4th 1960 the Mayor of Londonderry Nova Scotia – Senator J.G. Colhoun unveiled a cairn commemorating these settlers who build the township of Londonderry, Onslow and Truro.

Fulton LOL, Nova Scotia

West Dublin United Church, Nova Scotia

In Autumn 1762 some 170 more Ulster settlers came into Halifax on the same two ships and a significant section of this group settled in the New Dublin area of present day Lunenburg County.

In the Spring of 1763 McNutt returned to London in order to attempt to revive his fortunes but to no avail. In 1764 he was operating in Pennsylvania but this didn't work out either and shortly afterwards in 1765 he and his brother Benjamin received a grant of land in the Shelburne area where they established themselves on McNutt's Island. For the next thirty years Alexander McNutt split his time between this home and Truro. Thereafter he returned to Lexington Virginia where he died unmarried in 1811.

Another very significant Scots Irish settler who came to Nova Scotia shortly after McNutt was James 'Judge' Fulton.

George Archibald

He was born in Belfast in 1739 and emigrated to New England around 1760. He worked there as a surveyor. He arrived in Nova Scotia in 1765 and two years later was living in the Londonderry township. Shortly afterwards he as appointed as a J.P. for the area and thus started a professional career that would culminate in his appointment as a Judge of the Inferior Court of Common Pleas for Colchester. In 1793 he was commissioned as a Captain of the local Militia. By now Fulton's public persona was such that he was elected to the House of Assembly in 1799. In the period leading up to his election Fulton had been very involved in the formation of the 'Country Party'. This political grouping was formed as an alliance against the powerful Halifax Merchants. These individuals had built up their position and were perceived as being 'in cahoots' with the Privy Council and the Lieutenant Governor Sir John Wentworth. Fulton was amongst those who believed that their plan was to develop Halifax as a city at the expense of the surrounding countryside. Once elected Fulton maintained an independent streak and sometimes voted with the opposition rather than his own party. He spent his latter days in the Bass River area where he died in 1826. He had seven sons and eight daughters and in 1875 his great grandson George Fulton founded the Dominion Chair Company.

No account of Ulster Scots families in Nova Scotia would be complete without consideration of the Archibald family. Matthew Archibald was born in Londonderry in 1745 and settled in Truro Nova Scotia in 1762, being amongst those Ulster Scots who travelled up from their 'interim' stop in Londonderry New Hampshire. A bill of sale for 29th July 1779 which was registered in the Colchester County register of deeds shows him working as a tanner in Truro and purchasing for £50 from Mathew Harris of Pictou a slave boy of about 12 years old called 'Abram'. Abram was the son of Harris' slave in his former home in Maryland. Ownership of black slaves is not often a consideration whenever settlement in 18th century Nova Scotia is considered. Matthew Archibald was a member of the Assembly for Truro Township from 1785 until 1799. The later generation of the Archibald family who were born in Nova Scotia included Samuel George Archibald who became Chief Justice of Prince Edward Island and Sir Adams George Archibald who was born near Truro in 1814. He was elected as one of the delegates to the conferences in Quebec, Charlottetown and London which created the Confederation of Canada. On 1st July 1865 he became Secretary of State for Canada. Amongst many other high public offices he was later to become Lieutenant Governor of Manitoba and Lieutenant Governor of Nova Scotia. He died in Truro on 14th December 1892.

Other significant Ulster Scots families who settled in Nova Scotia include the McLellan family, the Vance family and the Rath family who lived at Hilden in the Province.

One indication of the strength of Ulster Scots settlement in Nova Scotia is evidenced in the growth of the Orange Order in the Province. The Order was particularly strong around the town of Westville. By the 1890's Orangemen were so active in this area that they were able to publish their own weekly newspaper. The longest serving Grand Master was William Caldwell who held the position from 1859 until 1872. In 1914 there were 127 lodges throughout Nova Scotia – from Glace Bay on Cape Breton Island to Yarmouth at the southern tip.

In more recent times Nova Scotians of Ulster Scots origin have included Robert L. Stanfield who was Premier of the Province from 1956 until 1967 and who challenged Pierre Trudeau for the Canadian Premiership in 1974 remaining Leader of the Opposition until 1976. Although Conservative in his political ideology he was a strong supporter of a bilingual Canada. He died on December 16th 2003 and is commemorated in the Halifax - Robert L Stanfield Airport which was so named in his honour in February of this current year. At the ceremony the Prime Minister of the Province, Stephen Harper described him as, "the best Prime Minister Canada never had".

Robert Stanfield

Plaque at Halifax Airport

Poems

Introduction to Poems

THESE little free verse poems tell something of a major exodus in my own family when Elisabeth Sheppard McReynolds and her two sons James and Joseph and their sister Elisabeth left Killyman Co Tyrone where they were members of the Society of Friends at nearby Grange Meeting. The year was 1737 and they travelled to Lancaster Pennsylvania as indentured servants and settled there to work off their indenture before heading to Virginia, Tennessee and North Carolina. They became Presbyterians in the Whitefieldian Revival and were baptized by Gilbert Tennent into that church. Thus began the story of many of the McReynolds family in the United States. I belong to the part of the family who did not go to America but stayed behind. It seemed a bit self-indulgent to me to include the family's history in prose so I wrote the poems to be little vignettes or windows through time that allow glimpses of the McReynolds family story and the motivation and struggle of the members of the family who took part in the events that are portrayed. I hope they succeed in giving an insight into a story that was not particularly remarkable but was rather typical of the Scots Irish emigrant experience.

THE VIEW FROM HERE

How different this Irish sounds
From the Gaelic of my own Argyle
And yet I understand but
Cannot speak it.
Here in Tyrone you don't
Need to know that
Liscausey means
'The fort by the wickerwork bridge'
Or that Ballyclog stands for
'The townland of the bell'
Its enough to list these townlands
At a stroll –
To know where you're going
And where you've been.
Ardtrea and Gortigal
Cloghog and Meenagh
Coash, Edernagh and Ballymaguire
In the middle stands the Brigh
Which is the name us Scots
Have given to the brow of this hill.

THE MILL AT CLONOE

Streaming water
Channelled from beyond the Brigh
And trundled here
Turns the breast wheel.
These locals sullenly marvel
At my skills
And yet I learned my way of working
On the killing side.
Metal and stone and rope
Now conjure grain and toss it
Water runs brown and mossy
As a trout's back
Where once the turf was bloodened.

MARY PRESTON'S GRAVESIDE - - - 1712

This old church
Has stood amongst the cows here
For two centuries and more,
Previously thatched and made of stone
Gazing nonchalantly out on a landscape
That Saint Patrick knew
Out across the western shore of Lough Neagh
From where I stand by your grave
Still as a stone
Numb and very dark very cold.

ELIZABETH'S STORY

I first glanced him
When he came to speak
With the four troopers
Who were billeted
With us.
He wasn't rough or rude
As they were
Grabbing – pushing against the wall.

My father knew him
Liked him
Knew men like him
Back in Durham
Men who had fought with Cromwell
Then turned a different path
Seeking the light.

His lisp was that of a stranger
He knew the Scotch language better,
For all his gentleness
And recently buried his wife
I knew there was a strength there
Of bone and muscle of mind
His dark looks his eyes
His smile was lethal.

CLOGHOG

Let me be honest with myself
Do I sit easily with these plain people?
All the way from Inverary
Me with my long *dirk of a name
Angular and sharp and guttural of tongue
Amongst these whose smooth handles
I can hardly lift
Nicholson and Whitsitt
Pim, Hobson, and Greaves
Sheppard and Greer I can manage
But Seaton and Millhouse
Slip from my grasp.

Down here in Tyrone
Where the sparrow-hawk and the *witterick
And the fox
Much close by
(And though my sons think it's an old soldier's madness)
I will build a nest amongst
These exotic gentle birds
This colony of soft spoken clerks
Who will record me in their minutes
Organise my day
Travel with me to meetings
Across in Ballyhagen and Ballinacree
And best of all
Secure me on a page in their
Book of Sufferings.

*dirk = *Scottish dagger*
*witterick = *Irish vernacular for a weasel or stoat*

QUAKER MEETING – GRANGE NEAR CHARLEMONT – CO. TYRONE

Silence
Save the wind swish of the tall ash trees
How strange to just sit here
Frozen
Not altogether comfortable
And yet how right
Righter than words I have known
A stranger
I glance around
Then turn within
To plunge the depths.

A MATTER OF PUBLIC RECORD

In memory of Johne McRannals

How did you fall
So suddenly
So powerfully calm?
To willingly put on such a drab garb
Bearing the outsider's mark
And adopting Quaker ways
You who had been
On the hill
Within the walls of Derry
And had soldiered in Flanders and beyond
Was it skinning the rat for your supper?
Or some more dreadful flashback image –
The maggot-filled head
Of a young boy in a mossy ditch,
Or did your old bones just grow tired?
Was it Elizabeth
Who shepherded you old ram?
Whatever it was it worked for a time
Before you lost your footing and fell from the ledge.
The shame
Hundreds of years later
Tickles and irritates
In my head
Sitting in the Public Records Office
I nip and tuck
And fold the page over
To keep the details penned in.

KILLYMAN FARM – REVISITED

A concrete path leads in now
With skinny grey beeches
In a guard of honour up both sides
I unwind the twine securing the gate
And drive in
With my latest batch of American 'cousins' on board.
I show them the cowshed
Where the dwelling house stood
And the hay barn
Which looks shocked – nay stunned
To be photographed so many times
And from so many angles
I explain that the old maps show that
The original path
Actually swung in a loop
Around the back field
And that was the way
Elizabeth McCrannolls
Her sons and daughter
Walked down with their little bundles
On the first stage of their journey
To Pennsylvania
Suddenly from out of a small
Dry closet at one end of a shed
The present owner Mr McFarland
Emerges from his newspaper and his tea
I've met him before in these circumstances
"If there's any money in it keep me in mind," he jokes
The 'cousins' are surprised that the place
Could now be owned by someone else
For in their photographs back in Tennessee
This shed and this barn
Will always belong to them.

GRIERSON'S RIDE THROUGH MISSISSIPPI – REVISITED

One October Sunday
Sunlight glinting sideways
Through the trunks
We drove through the woods
Missing birch poles by inches
To see the old family tannery
Famed for making boots
For the Confederacy,
Close by an old log house
Where four McReynolds brothers
Taught school
At different times
A hundred years ago or more,
We drove to the spot where Grierson
Came through
On his ride.

It's said that his troopers
Took no retribution
Because they were so well
Fed and watered,
Out here in rural
Oktibbeha County
Or 'cold bloody water'
As it is in Choctaw
I expected to see
Wallsteads and buildings,
But instead find
Only the declivities
Of the tanning vats
Hollows bowls
Dried eye sockets
In the face of
The crumbly leafy earth.

MARTINSBURG ROAD

Now at fifty three
I have trained
My men
Not to change forwards
As Kearney and I
And one hundred dragoons
Did at Chirabusco.

Here in West Virginia
With massive brigade weight
Creaking and clanking
We up and leave
Campfire embers burning
Beans heating in the pot.

Yesterday they brought
A captured Reb. Before me
“Where are you from?”
I asked him
“I’m from Dungannon
Like yourself Sir.”

REEDS VALLEY VIRGINIA – THE FALL 1998

Only a pile of boards
And the well remains
Reflecting the brown and orange and yellow
From the maple and the hickory
The sinister 'conkers' of black walnuts
Lie all around like grapeshot.

"One of your kin,"
My guide informs me,
"Hid from the Yankees
When they came through
During the Civil War
Up in a cave in the hills there
Spent his time weaving baskets
Into all kinds of shapes,"
It seems he made
A kind of slipe
To pull behind the horse
And carry four children in.

Predictably I feel at home here
Where these country folk
Kept bees, grew tobacco
And were baptised
Close by in the Clinch river.

THE VISITOR FROM WASHINGTON

Naught but a scant trace now
Of their names
On the old Concord church records
And yet other accounts
Show James and Mary
After their baptism by Gilbert Tennent
Sitting on the pews
Inside these walls
With Hester and Caeser
Almost as equals.

I'm lightened by this journey here today
Even though there is
Little real recognition left
Of who they were,
I have arranged
With the minister
To have the old pulpit Bible
And the Kirk Session record book
Strengthened with wooden pattens
And bound with leather.

Select Bibliography

Unpublished Theses

Barry, William David, *Bryce McLellan and His Children,* unpublished thesis in Maine Historical Society, Portland Maine.

Barry, William David and Holverson, John, *The Revolutionary McLellans,* unpublished thesis in Maine Historical Society, Portland Maine.

Osborne, Mary J. McMahon,*Rea of Ballynahinch Holywood &Allied Families,* unpublished thesis in Public Reference Office, Belfast, N.Ireland.Ref. PRONI. D/3000/149.

Published Books And Articles

Abbot, Herman, *History of Belfast.*

Bailyn, Bernard,*Pamphlets of the American Revolution, 1756-1776.*

Bailyn, Bernard,*The Peopling of British North America.*

Baker, Jean H., *The Stevensons.*

Barefield, Shawn, A., and Holt, Brian, R., *Old Town- The Forgotten Years 1780-1810.*

Bernard, Shane,*Tabasco:An Illustrated History*

Brown, D. Alexander, *Grierson's Raid, A Cavalry Adventure of the Civil War.*

Brown, Michael, *Francis Hutcheson in Dublin.*

Brown, William L.Jr., *Revolutionary Spirit, A view of the Scotch-Irish Influence in America.*

Chase, Henry, *Governor John Pinckney Dunlap.*

Conforti, Joseph A., *Creating Portland-History and Place in Northern New England.*

Connolly, Michael, C. (ed), *They Change Their Sky: The Irish in Maine.*

Covici, Pascal, Jr. (ed), *The Portable Steinbeck.*

Dangerfield, George, *The Awakening of American Nationalism.*

Dickson, R. J., *Ulster Emigration to Colonial America.*

Doyle, David Noel, *Ireland,Irishmen and Revolutionary America.*

Fischer, David Hackett, *Albion's Seed.*

Fitzpatrick, Rory, *God's Frontiersmen: The Scots-Irish Epic.*

Ford Henry James, *The Scotch Irish in America.*

Green, E.R.R., *Queensborough, Township: Scotch Irish Emigration and the Expansion of Georgia 1763-1776.* In William and Mary Quarterly, 3rd Ser., Vol XVII no.2, April 1960.

Hutcheson, Francis, *An Inquiry into the Origins of Our Ideas of Beauty and Virtue.*

Kellogg Elijah, *Good Old Times.*
Leyburn, James G., *The Scotch Irish-A Social History.*
Macrory, Patrick, *The Siege of Derry.*
Mann, John T., *Ulster Scots on the Coast of Maine.*
Martin, James Kirby, et al, *America and its People,* Volume One-To 1877
Michener, James A., *The Eagle and The Raven.*
Miller, Kerby A. (ed), *Irish Immigrants in the Land of Canaan,* Letters and Memoirs from Colonial and Revolutionary America, 1675-1815.
Montgomery, Dennis, *1607, Jamestown and the New World.*
Myers, Albert Cook, *Immigration of the Irish Quakers into Pennsylvania.*
McCartney, D.J., *The Ulster Jacksons.*
McGee Thomas D'Arcy, *A History of the Irish settlers in North America.*
Newmann, Kate, *Dictionary of Ulster Biography.*
O'Brien, M.J., *The Lost Town of Cork/ME.*
Oliver, J.A., *Some Ulster Scots and their Origins in Scotland.* In Familia, Vol 2, no.3, pages 96-110.
Parker, Rev.Edward L., *History of Londonderry NH.*
Perry, Rev. A. L., *Scotch Irish in New England.*
Peters M.D., De Witt C., *The Life and Adventures of Kit Carson the Nestor of The Rocky Mountains from facts narrated by himself.*
Raulston, J.Leonard and Livingood, James W., *Sequatchie, A Story of the Southern Cumberlands.*
Roulston, William, *Reconstructing an eighteenth-century Ulster family: the Reas of Magheraknock and Killeen, County Down.* In Familia (2004), pp 85-94.
Sides, Hampton, *Blood and Thunder.*
Steinbeck, John, *America and Americans.* Chapter entitled, I Go Back to Ireland.1953.
Steinbeck, John, *East of Eden.*
Taylor, Alan, *The Divided Ground.Indians, Settlers and the Northern Borderland of the American Revolution.*
Varney, George J., *History of Belfast Maine.*
Whalen, Charles and Barbara, *The Fighting McCooks.*
Williamson, Joseph, *History of Belfast.*
Wills,Garry, *Inventing America - Jefferson's Declaration of Independence*
Woodard, Colin, *The Lobster Coast.*

Websites

A word about the internet.
Although it is important to be careful, there is an increasing number of valuable sources available online. I have used these extensively but with care. If I have not noted or acknowledged any material gathered in this way

let me apologise in advance. I am somewhat reluctant to list websites, due to the evanescence of the medium, but here is a list of some of the sites which proved useful in preparing this book.

http://genforum.genealogy.com/galphin/messages/5.html

www.genealogylinks.net/uk/ireland/down

http://genforum.genealogy.com/muse/messages/812html

http://www.georgiaencyclopedia.org/nge/Home.jsp

http://homepages.rootsweb.com/~merle/History/SI-NE.htm

http://isabelvandervelde.com/blank.html

http://www.Isjunction.com/people/houston.htm

http://www.kansasheritage.org/families/kitcarson.html

http://www.libraryireland.com/articles/ScotchIrishNewEnglandCongress1890/index.php

http://www.libraryireland.com/ScotchIrishAmericaIXII.2php

http://1718migration.org.uk/s_thesearchforAhome.asp

http://www.downcountymuseum.com/uploads/2000_Orr_Mr_Hutcheson.doc.

'The Ingenious Mr Hutcheson' - An essay on a neglected Scots-Irishman by Philip Orr.

Index of Names and Places

Alister McReynolds
(Photography by Kirsty)

Alister McReynolds
LEGACY

ALISTER MCREYNOLDS has written extensively on Scots Irish history and culture and in particular about the achievements of the diaspora in the United States.

As an educator McReynolds is doubly qualified as a librarian and also as a teacher. However his career of over thirty years has been spent largely as the latter - a teacher. In 1994 his teaching career culminated in his appointment as a College Principal in his native Ulster. He held this post successfully for 14 years before deciding on a change of direction. Since then he has lectured at many venues across the United States, including at The Smithsonian Institute in Washington D.C.

Articles have been published in numerous journals including, The Ulster Scotsman and The Pine Tree Highlander as well as in The Belfast Telegraph and The Newsletter.

He has appeared in BBC local history television and radio programmes and acted as a commentator and consultant on Scots Irish matters for various media projects.

Alister McReynolds obtained his initial and higher degrees as well as his postgraduate qualifications from Queen's University Belfast and The University of Ulster. McReynolds is also an Honorary Member of City and Guilds of London Institute - an award that recognised his contribution to vocational education in Northern Ireland. He has also been awarded the position of, Fellow of the Society of Antiquaries of Scotland.

In August 2007 he was given a prestigious Honorary Research Fellowship with the Institute of Ulster Scots Studies at The University of Ulster.

He resides in Magheragall, Co. Antrim with his wife Eileen and has a daughter Kirsty, and two sons Michael and Alex.